A Wilder Life

A Wilder Life

A Season-by-Season Guide to Getting in Touch with Nature

CELESTINE MADDY
with Abbye Churchill

NEW YORK

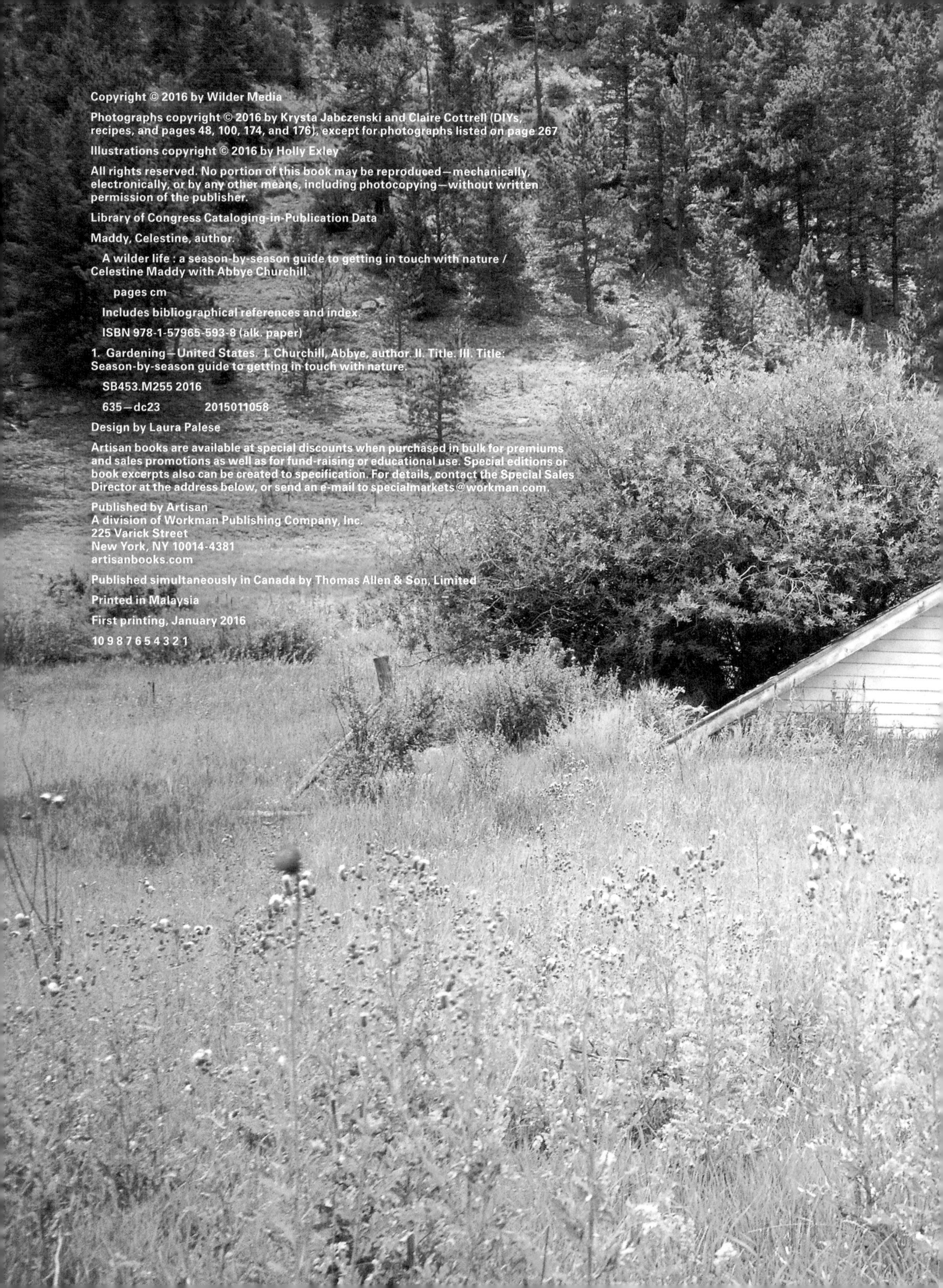

Library of Congress Cataloging-in-Publication Data

Maddy, Celestine, author.

A wilder life : a season-by-season guide to getting in touch with nature / Celestine Maddy with Abbye Churchill.

pages cm

Includes bibliographical references and index.

ISBN 978-1-57965-593-8 (alk. paper)

1. Gardening—United States. I. Churchill, Abbye, author. II. Title. III. Title: Season-by-season guide to getting in touch with nature.

SB453.M255 2016

635—dc23 2015011058

Design by Laura Palese

Artisan books are available at special discounts when purchased in bulk for premiums and sales promotions as well as for fund-raising or educational use. Special editions or book excerpts also can be created to specification. For details, contact the Special Sales Director at the address below, or send an e-mail to specialmarkets@workman.com.

Published by Artisan
A division of Workman Publishing Company, Inc.
225 Varick Street
New York, NY 10014-4381
artisanbooks.com

Published simultaneously in Canada by Thomas Allen & Son, Limited

Printed in Malaysia

First printing, January 2016

10 9 8 7 6 5 4 3 2 1

CONTENTS

SPRING

SUMMER

FALL

WINTER

INTRODUCTION

It is not enough to fight for the land; it is even more important to enjoy it. While you can. While it's still here. So get out there and hunt and fish and mess around with your friends, ramble out yonder and explore the forests, climb the mountains, bag the peaks, run the rivers, breathe deep of that yet sweet and lucid air, sit quietly for a while and contemplate the precious stillness, the lovely, mysterious, and awesome space. Enjoy yourselves, keep your brain in your head and your head firmly attached to the body, the body active and alive, and I promise you this much; I promise you this one sweet victory over our enemies, over those desk-bound men and women with their hearts in a safe deposit box, and their eyes hypnotized by desk calculators. I promise you this; You will outlive the bastards.

—**EDWARD ABBEY (1927–1989)**

Ask anyone who knew me in my early twenties if they could have imagined I'd grow up to be a champion of the great outdoors. Not one would say yes. I have a feeling a few would laugh. I wouldn't fault them. I am a lover of the city life, a fast walker, a loud talker, a night owl, and an urban devotee. I want all the amenities and experiences. I want the most of everything and I want it all the time, right now. It's one reason I love technology. It's instant gratification. I often have a hard time choosing between an evening spent surfing the Internet and one spent playing a video game.

Until a few years ago, the natural world felt like an abstraction to me. I thought of nature as only those places featured on cable programs narrated by a rich, booming voice that I would later learn to cherish as David Attenborough's. "Nature" was in the pages of big, heavy books and thin magazines laced with lifestyle ads. It appeared on screen savers and outside car windows, whizzing by on one of my rare half-day Fridays when I would escape the office after working twelve-hour days several days in a row.

But in my late twenties, things changed. I began to cultivate a part of myself that had remained undiscovered. I had just moved in with my then boyfriend, now husband. He was the proud renter of a diamond in the rough—a brownstone with a backyard. I found a new kind of peace among my freshly planted hostas and toad lilies. I could exhale and be still. I went from sweating it out on the front stoop to spending hot afternoons knee-deep in soil and confusion. I drowned plants; I forgot to water others. I killed countless innocent seedlings in my mission to connect and comprehend nature.

That plot of land off of Flatbush Avenue in Brooklyn helped me move nature from the esoteric to the very real. I realized that nature is everywhere—it's where we live, breathe, and eat. Nature is on my friend John's rooftop and in my mother's suburban backyard. It's a few feet away from you when you step out your front door, and it's a few hundred miles away, too, when you travel afar. It's where our food is grown and where we go to take a dip in cool waters on hot days. As we move farther from the green bits (the bright flowers, the big trees) and closer to the bytes and our glowing screens, I think we all find ourselves searching for balance between these seemingly oppositional worlds.

Wilder, the magazine, began in 2011 as a place to connect the dots between twenty-first-century living and the slow pace of the great outdoors. Over the years of publishing the magazine, we have redefined the conversation to focus on the growing and natural world. And *A Wilder Life* is a companion to that experience. Abbye Churchill, *Wilder*'s editorial director; Molly Marquand, *Wilder*'s horticultural editor; and I, the founder of *Wilder,* have pooled our collective experience to give you the basic knowledge you need to move from bystander to doer, at home and in the wild.

The book is organized by season—spring, summer (my personal favorite), fall, and winter—and gives you appropriate seasonal activities for each. In order to help you navigate the 272 pages of essential knowledge in *A Wilder Life,* each season has been further separated into five categories of knowledge: growing, cooking, home and self-reliance, beauty and healing, and wilderness. Each section begins with a checklist to help you prepare for and enjoy the season, ranging from tasks to do in the garden to how to stock your pantry to create the season's culinary delights. From here, you can discover the joys and the nuisances, along with the good-to-knows and the how-tos that make each season a unique pleasure. Learn to craft with the bounty of the wild, take a trip to some of the most inspiring gardens on earth, make your own perfume, build an outdoor shelter, or navigate by reading the stars. *A Wilder Life* contains recipes, DIYs, skills, and guides that we consider the foundations for amazing natural experiences. We've also asked experts like auteur David Lynch, beauty expert Brenda Brock, and our own mothers for their tricks and tools for making the outdoors your very own.

My hope is that this book finds its way off your coffee table and into your backyard and your backpack. Use *A Wilder Life* as your tool and as a guide. Move beyond what you know and into your own exploration of the bright-eyed world all around you.

There are photos, empty matchboxes, flyers from shows, mementos, and memories pinned across my bedroom wall. As we were putting this book to bed, I added the galvanizing words of Edward Abbey, noted American author, naturalist, and environmental activist, to the collection. He wrote and said a million wonderful things, but my favorite energizes me upon each reading. I hope this book does the same for you.

Spring

THE FIRST HINT OF SPRING MAKES YOU REJOICE.

The snow begins to melt away. The sun becomes less of a savior from bitter winds and freezing fingers and more of a cheerful companion ushering us into a bountiful season. The spring equinox brings with it the early blooming flowers, such as the iris and the hyacinth. The warmth of those first days also brings worms, bugs, and bees to life. They stir just beneath the warming soil. And just like with nature, spring breathes new life into each of us. Stretch out your arms and take in a deep breath. Uncurl your limbs and shake off the quiet, pleasant numbness of winter. It's time to be of the natural world once again. As Tolstoy said, "Spring is the time of plans and projects."

No matter if you're in living in a buzzing city center or in peaceful rural seclusion, spring is a time to build a foundation for the seasons to come. Start seeds indoors to ensure that you have strong seedlings ready to be planted by the end of spring (see page 27 for step-by-step instructions). Honey lovers can get busy with beekeeping (see page 50), and on spring days that are still cold, try your hand at working with natural dyes (see page 49).

Springtime is a season of discovery. Spend your mornings wild crafting in a local public park or a nearby forest to seek out the edible and medicinal plants as they push forth into the light. Dandelion and beach rose are our favorite finds. The former makes an excellent tincture (see page 63) for liver health, and the latter, with its pungent, rich aroma, can be made into a perfume. If you happen to be anywhere near the Netherlands, now is the time to take a jaw-dropping twenty-five-mile drive past fields of flowers: tulips, dahlias, lilies—all of the classic Dutch bulbs on display. Those on North America's Pacific coastline can marvel at the sight of whales pushing through the open sea as they head to warmer waters. All around the world, nature offers up spectacular viewing in springtime.

SPRING

GROWING

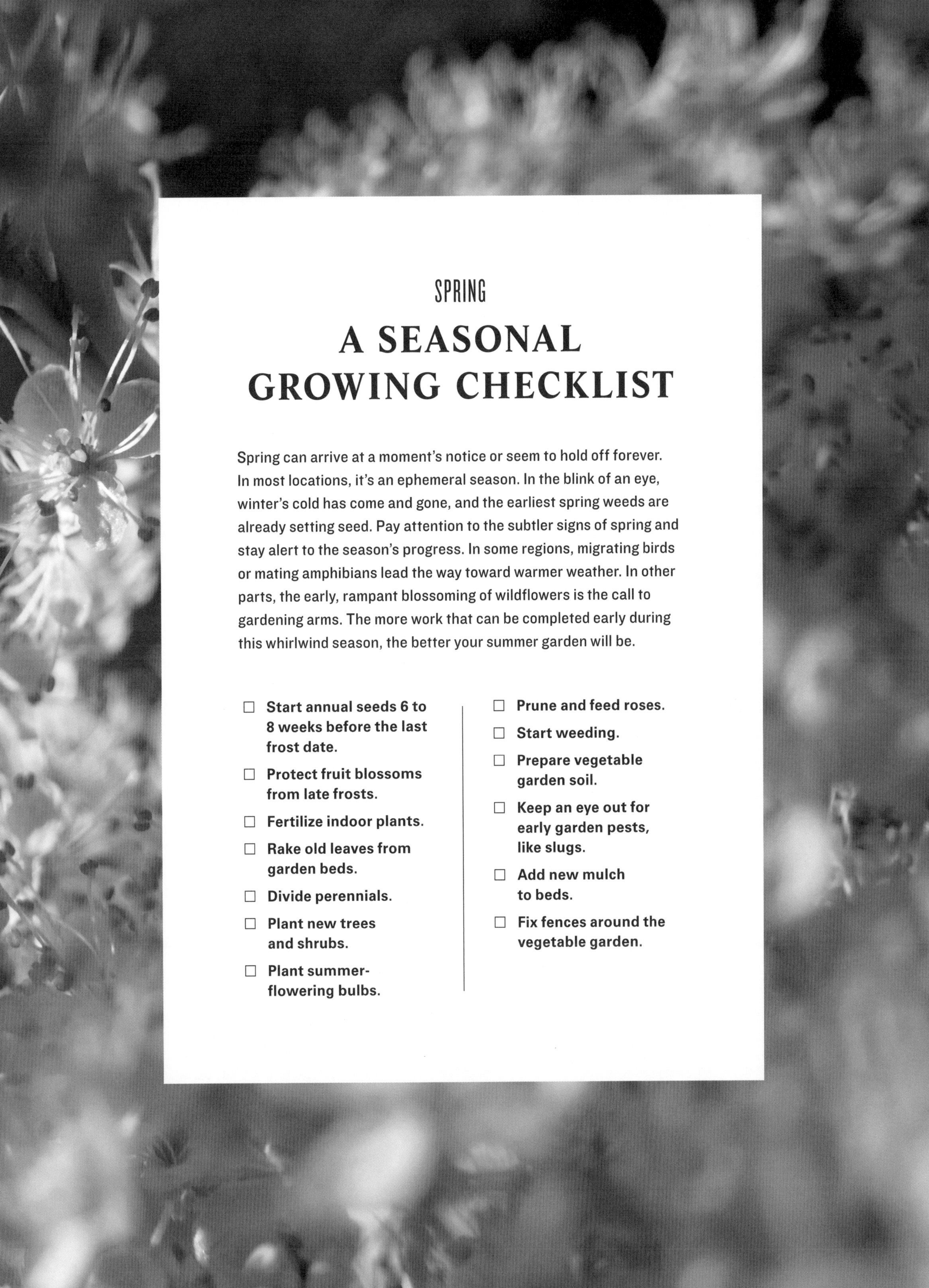

SPRING

A SEASONAL GROWING CHECKLIST

Spring can arrive at a moment's notice or seem to hold off forever. In most locations, it's an ephemeral season. In the blink of an eye, winter's cold has come and gone, and the earliest spring weeds are already setting seed. Pay attention to the subtler signs of spring and stay alert to the season's progress. In some regions, migrating birds or mating amphibians lead the way toward warmer weather. In other parts, the early, rampant blossoming of wildflowers is the call to gardening arms. The more work that can be completed early during this whirlwind season, the better your summer garden will be.

- ☐ **Start annual seeds 6 to 8 weeks before the last frost date.**
- ☐ **Protect fruit blossoms from late frosts.**
- ☐ **Fertilize indoor plants.**
- ☐ **Rake old leaves from garden beds.**
- ☐ **Divide perennials.**
- ☐ **Plant new trees and shrubs.**
- ☐ **Plant summer-flowering bulbs.**
- ☐ **Prune and feed roses.**
- ☐ **Start weeding.**
- ☐ **Prepare vegetable garden soil.**
- ☐ **Keep an eye out for early garden pests, like slugs.**
- ☐ **Add new mulch to beds.**
- ☐ **Fix fences around the vegetable garden.**

COMMON NAME
Liverleaf

LATIN NAME
Hepatica acutiloba

BLOOM TIME
Early spring

LIGHT
Part to full shade

SOIL
Moist, rich, neutral soil

PESTS & PROBLEMS
Generally disease free; occasionally affected by leaf miners

BEST USE
Dense drifts on woodland slopes

PLANT PROFILE

LIVERLEAF

Best enjoyed in blowsy drifts of purple and white, the North American liverleaf is an easy-to-grow spring ephemeral well suited to the woodland garden. Emerging from beneath piles of winter leaves, liverleaf is one of the year's first bloomers. A close relative of the buttercup, the liverleaf shares the same artless, open blooms of the family, although unlike buttercups, the cultivated varieties are commonly purple to blue. Clusters of rich yellow stamens ring the delicate flower's center, adding more interest and color. Plant liverleaf on woodland slopes and along forest trails. It is an excellent naturalizer. As the seasons shift, liverleaf's violet blossoms will slash through the last dregs of wintry murk and get spring springing on its way.

Seeds

Cold stratified seeds will readily germinate outdoors in spring. If sowing in pots or trays indoors, start plants in early spring, eight weeks before the final frost date. This way, they'll be ready for transplanting as soon as the weather warms. Make sure the soil remains moist until germination occurs.

Root Cuttings

Root cuttings are an easy way to propagate liverleaf. Divide roots with a sterilized, sharp knife to prevent infection and tearing. Plant the cuttings directly outside with the point of growth facing upward.

Young Plants

Liverleaf takes approximately two years to bloom when grown from seed. Bear in mind that young plants may require additional watering when first planted to speed establishment and growth.

Mature Plants

Mature, flowering individuals require lots of water during the spring months. After flowers have withered at the end of spring, the plants' old leaves may rapidly brown. Snip off old leaves with pruners or scissors to make way for new green growth next spring.

PLANT PROFILE

WILD HYACINTH

When swaths of wild hyacinths bloom clear across western North America, fields mirror summer skies. The light blue flowers look as beautiful in the garden as they do in the wild—blooming in oceanic-scale profusion. Statuesque summer-flowering bulbs, wild hyacinths grow up to four feet tall, so make sure to give them ample space. Relied upon as a staple food source by the Salish, Blackfeet, and Nez Percé Indians of the North American west, wild hyacinth bulb tastes somewhat like sweet potato when cooked. To harvest the bulbs, wait until autumn, after the flowers have withered, and roast in the oven or over the fire.

Seeds

Although wild hyacinth can be grown from seed, it takes three or more years for the small seeds to mature into flowering bulbs. Seeds can be collected during July and August, and perform best when sown directly outside, or into a cold frame the following spring. Germination will occur within one to six months.

Bulbs

Small bulblets are best collected from the mother bulb in midsummer, during the plant's dormancy. Gently pry off the small bulbs and replant about four inches deep and six inches apart in rich, moist soil.

Young Plants

Young plants require little attention if out in the garden. If growing them in pots, be sure to keep soil moist and lightly fertilized.

Mature Plants

Mature individuals are incredibly hardy, and will tolerate a range of soil types without fertilization. In general, however, wild hyacinths prefer freely draining soils rich in nutrients. If given sufficient space and moisture, wild hyacinth will steadily reproduce over time, expanding into large and handsome swaths of flowers that bloom reliably each and every year.

COMMON NAME

Wild hyacinth

LATIN NAME

Camassia quamash

BLOOM TIME

Early summer

LIGHT

Part shade to full sun

SOIL

Rich, well-drained, acidic

PESTS & PROBLEMS

Few

BEST USE

Perfume, as each of its colors offers a separate, distinct aroma

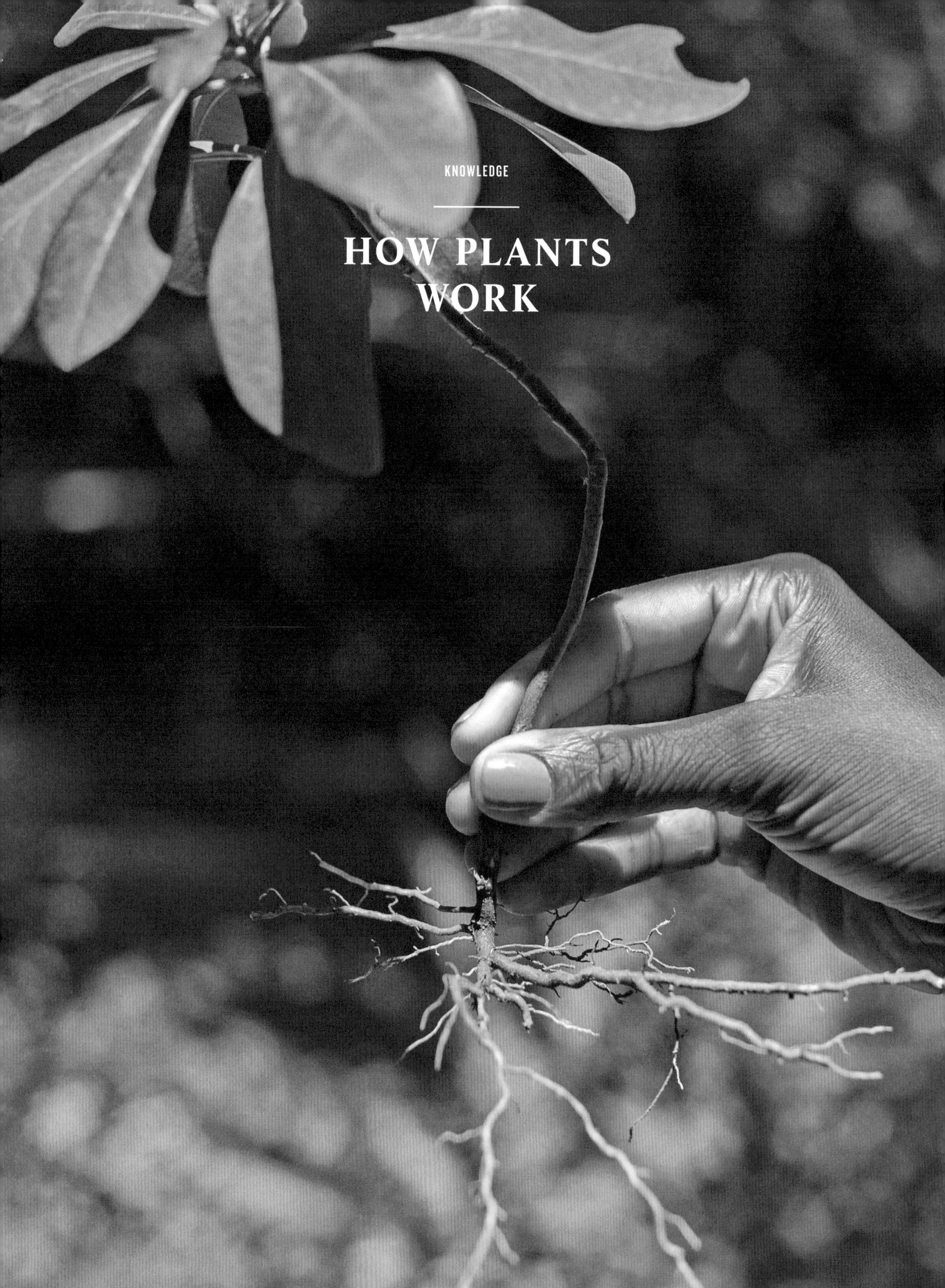

KNOWLEDGE

HOW PLANTS WORK

In biology, form follows function. The large, umbrella-shaped leaves of shade plants capture light filtering through the crowded jungle canopy, while the compact nubs of succulent foliage store a precious cache of water. All the way down the taxonomic tree, plants have evolved mechanisms to get done what needs doing: spines, barbs, and irritating hairs protect against herbivory; bulbs, corms, and tubers lock up important nutrients; and myriad flowers tend to that most crucial of all biological acts, reproduction.

Leaves are the site of a plant's two vital functions: transpiration and photosynthesis. As oxygen and carbon are exchanged via the leaf's delicate membrane, sunlight is captured and turned into energy. For this reason, it's important to keep leaves dust free and exposed to an appropriate amount of fuel-supplying sun.

The plant's stem is the steward of buds and one of the sources of new growth. It's also the transport system for water and food. Some plants, like cacti, use their stem to store food, while others, like crocus, keep it buried underground. In either case, the stem is an important stabilizing structure, and must be kept sturdy and healthy in order to perform its functions. Appropriate sunlight and moisture will ensure that stems do not grow thin and weedy or weaken and rot.

Roots are a plant's anchor. They're also responsible for nutrient and water uptake. Interference with the delicate root hairs that make up much of the root system's absorbent surface are often the cause for flagging plant health—if roots become waterlogged, they drown, stopping nutrient exchange. When transplanting seedlings or divided clumps, remember the fragile root hairs, and provide extra love and care until new hairs have time to regrow.

KNOW YOUR PLANT VOCABULARY

Knowing the correct terms is essential to knowing your plants. Speak plant and watch your relationship with them grow.

CORM: an underground stem used to store food

INFLORESCENCE: a cluster of flowers

MERISTEM: plant tissue that produces new growth

PHOTOSYNTHESIS: the process by which a plant captures sunlight and uses it to synthesize food

PISTIL: the female reproductive organs of a flower that receive the pollen

SEPAL: the protective tissue that covers a budded flower's petals prior to opening

STIPULE: a structure found at the base of certain plants' leaves

STAMEN: the male, pollen-producing reproductive organs of a flower

STOMATA: tiny openings on the leaves where gas exchange takes place

TRANSPIRATION: the process by which a plant loses water through pores on the leaf surface

TURGOR: rigidity of cells due to water absorption

SKILL

HOW TO GROW FROM SEEDS

In essence, starting seeds is simple: tuck a seed beneath the dirt and, with a little bit of luck, something will grow. In reality, seeds are finicky things and require lots of patience and attention. To cut down on seedling losses and increase germination rates, invest in nutritious sterilized potting mix. If you're just starting out, plant seeds that are surefire growers, like cosmos and sweet peas.

WHAT YOU'LL NEED

Seeds

Sharp knife

Bucket for mixing

Compost

Sand

Perlite

Peat moss

Seed trays

NOTE: Some very hard seeds like cup and saucer, nasturtium, and moonflower vine need to be soaked overnight or nicked with a knife prior to planting. Check the back of the seed packet for this information. Make sure to soak or nick all the seeds that need this extra help to ensure successful germination.

DIRECTIONS

1. In a bucket, mix together equal parts of finished compost, sand, perlite, and peat moss. Add water until the mixture is evenly moist.

2. Lightly tamp soil into seed trays or pots. (Shallow seed trays work best as moisture is more easily monitored in small containers.)

3. Gently brush 1 to 3 seedlings per container onto the surface of the soil and lightly cover with soil. A good rule of thumb is that each seed should be planted at a depth three times its width.

4. Place seed trays in a bright, sunny location and try to keep the temperature steady, around 65°F. Keep the soil moist, but not soaking. Rot is the fastest and easiest way to kill seedlings.

5. After the seeds have germinated, wait a week or two to see which will arise as the strongest in the pot. Pinch off the weaklings to give the fittest the best chance to grow. Allow them to develop two sets of "true" leaves before moving them. Once the danger of frost has passed, plant these seedlings out in your garden or in larger containers.

KNOWLEDGE

PLANT A NATIVE GARDEN

Naturally resilient to pests, pathogens, and the ever-changing weather, native plants are an obvious choice for the hands-off gardener. However, native plants are not just what is on offer at your local mass garden-center—natives come in a multitude of colors, forms, and fragrances for the greediest of garden kleptomaniacs. Pollinators love native plants, birds flock to feed on their seeds and fruit, and they'll lend a real sense of place to your home and garden. When choosing natives, think of their utility for each of the seasons. Native species are designed to carefully fit a special niche in the landscape, whether that is providing food for the first hummingbirds of the year or giving dense shelter to the last drifts of autumn butterflies as they migrate to their winter homes. Here are the steps to take to invite native species into your backyard.

1. Figure out the goals of the garden. Are butterflies, bees, or birds the intended focus? Does the garden need more winter interest or fruiting trees? See the following lists for help.

2. Understand the garden's environmental characteristics. Purchase a soil test kit from your local nursery and find out whether the soil is acidic, basic, or circumneutral. There are a host of native plants that are suitable for most types of soil.

3. Whether you're in the United Kingdom or the United States, be sure to know your garden's growing zone. These zones are determined based upon regional minimum temperatures and are the starting point to knowing what you can, and can't, grow. Topography, elevation, and aspect can all affect the microclimate of the garden. Look up which zone your garden falls into on the United States Department of Agriculture (USDA) website (see Resources, page 265) and spend some time learning about minimum and maximum temperatures in the local area. Although native plants are more tolerant than their exotic counterparts, not all of them are cold hardy.

Our Favorite Native Plants and Their Uses

All of these natives can be grown in several different zones across the world. They are particularly well suited to their region of origin, but are useful wherever they are planted.

NORTHEAST UNITED STATES

MAYAPPLE (*Podophyllum peltatum*): attracts turtles

SHADBUSH (*Amelanchier*): attracts birds; produces edible fruit

AMERICAN HAZELNUT (*Corylus americana*): attracts bears, squirrels, and other rodents; produces edible nuts

VIRGINIA SWITCHGRASS (*Panicum virgatum*): provides a winter habitat

GREAT LAUREL (*Rhododendron maximum*): provides a winter habitat; attracts butterflies

SOUTHEAST UNITED STATES

SWEETBAY MAGNOLIA (*Magnolia virginiana*): attracts bees and beetles

SWEETSHRUB (*Calycanthus floridus*): attracts bees and beetles

RATTLESNAKE MASTER (*Eryngium yuccifolium*): is a host plant for swallowtail butterflies

VIRGINIA BLUEBELLS (*Mertensia virginica*): attracts early pollinators and hummingbirds

YELLOW LOTUS (*Nelumbo lutea*): attracts beetles; produces edible seeds

MIDWEST UNITED STATES

OHIO BUCKEYE (*Aesculus glabra*): attracts bears, squirrels, and other rodents

GREEN-HEADED CONEFLOWER (*Rudebeckia laciniata*): attracts bees

PRAIRIE DROPSEED (*Sporobolus heterolepis*): provides a winter habitat

COMMON MILKWEED (*Asclepias syriaca*): attracts monarch butterflies

WESTERN SUNFLOWER (*Helianthus occidentalis*): attracts bees and butterflies

SOUTHWEST UNITED STATES

GREENLEAF MANZANITA (*Arctostaphylos patula*): attracts birds and bees; produces edible fruit

SCARLET GLOBE MALLOW (*Sphaeralcea coccinea*): attracts birds and small mammals; is a host plant for small-checkered skipper butterflies

THREADLEAF GIANT HYSSOP (*Agastache rupestris*): attracts hummingbirds and butterflies

ROCKY MOUNTAIN CLEMATIS (*Clematis pseudoalpina*): attracts bees and butterflies

GOLDEN BARREL CACTUS (*Echinocactus grusonii*): attracts bees; produces edible seeds for birds

SOUTHERN CALIFORNIA

BROADLEAF STONECROP (*Sedum spathulifolium*): attracts bees

BLUE SAGE (*Salvia clevelandii*): attracts bees and hummingbirds

PINELEAF PENSTEMON (*Penstemon pinifolius*): attracts bees, butterflies, and hummingbirds

PINK FLOWERING CURRANT (*Ribes sanguineum glutinosum*): attracts hummingbirds; produces edible fruit for wildlife

WESTERN DOGWOOD (*Cornus nuttallii*): attracts bees; host plant for blue azure butterfly; produces edible fruit for wildlife

PACIFIC NORTHWEST UNITED STATES

VINE MAPLE (*Acer circinatum*): is a host plant for brown tissue and polyhemous moths

WESTERN WILD GINGER (*Asarum caudatum*): produces edible roots and leaves

DEER FERN (*Blechnum spicant*): provides dense cover and forage for deer, mountain goats, and elk

INSIDE-OUT FLOWER (*Vancouveria hexandra*): attracts bees

BLUE COLUMBINE (*Aquilegia caerulea*): attracts hummingbirds and bees

SPRING

COOKING

SPRING

INGREDIENTS TO INSPIRE

Fruits

APRICOTS
APRIUMS
BLACKBERRIES (EARLY)
BLUEBERRIES (EARLY)
CHERRIES
FIGS (EARLY)
LEMONS
LOQUATS
MANDARINS
RASPBERRIES
RHUBARB
STRAWBERRIES

Vegetables

ARTICHOKES
ASPARAGUS (PURPLE AND GREEN)
BELGIAN ENDIVE
BROCCOLI
CACTUS
CHAYOTE SQUASH
CHIVES
COLLARD GREENS
FAVA BEANS
FENNEL
FIDDLEHEAD FERNS
GARLIC SCAPES
GREEN BEANS
LETTUCE
MUSHROOMS
MUSTARD GREENS
NETTLES
PEA PODS
PEAS
PURSLANE
RADICCHIO
RADISHES
RAMPS
SNOW PEAS
SORREL
SPINACH
SWISS CHARD
VIDALIA ONIONS
WATERCRESS

KNOWLEDGE

A PRIMER ON CHEESE MAKING

Odes have been written to it. It smothers our omelets and makes our hamburgers golden. Whole grocery store aisles are devoted to it, and countries claim it as their own. We are speaking, of course, of cheese.

How did this majestic coagulate come to be? Legends vary. For some (namely the Swiss), the story involves a wandering merchant traveling across the desert some five thousand years ago. The traveler was transporting some sheep's milk in a pouch made from the animal's hollowed-out stomach. The activity of travel agitated the milk, like churning, and when it combined with the naturally occurring rennet in the sheep's stomach, it turned into curds and whey. Others believe that in the process of salt-curdling milk for preservation, cheese was invented as a happy by-product. Evidence of cheese making can be found scrawled on ancient Egyptian tombs and in records of the Roman Empire. Though we may never know its exact origin story, cheese has come a long way since.

Cheeses Today

Grocery aisles are piled high with varieties of cheese sourced from around the world. Crumbly, buttery, milky, pungent, robust: it can be a dizzying experience to roam the cheese counter. That's why experts have developed—over hundreds of years—ways of classifying cheese, in order to bring method to this creamy madness.

- **FRESH:** uncooked, unaged, soft, and milky (ricotta and mozzarella are good examples)
- **SOFT-RIPENED:** semisoft and buttery with a white rind (for example, Brie)
- **WASHED-RIND:** semisoft cheeses that have been washed in water, wine, beer, or some other liquid to encourage bacteria growth (think Limburger)
- **NATURAL-RIND:** has a rind that forms without the additional inclusion of mold or bacteria (a favorite is English Stilton)
- **BLUE-VEINED:** marbled, semisoft to firm, with veins of cultures ranging from blue to green (Gorgonzola is a blue-veined cheese)
- **PRESSED:** curds are pressed together to form a dense texture; can be cooked or uncooked (cheddar, for example)

Each of these blooming, lovely varieties has developed to become its own distinct variety thanks to technical trial and error, difference in geographic location, and personal artistic proclivity.

How to Make Cheese

The basic equation of cheese, regardless of its myriad end forms, is the same: acidify milk to coagulate the curds (dense bits) from the whey (liquid). However, like any true artistry, it is in the nuances of this process that the real magic happens. Milk can be acidified using an acid like vinegar, lemon juice, or citric acid, or with a culture or bacteria to separate the curds. Rennet (an isolated enzyme found in the stomach lining of some mammals) can be added to curdle the casein, or proteins, in milk. From that point on, variances in process—from the type of milk, the introduction of water back into the curds, and how the whey is expelled from the curds to the heating process, stretching, smoking, aging, mold introduction, rind washing, and many other factors—will dictate the final form the cheese will take.

To learn more about the processes behind cheese making, we suggest you let your taste buds be your guide. Visit your local cheesemonger and ask to sample a few of the varieties listed above. Which are you attracted to? Which taste better to you? Do you prefer the stink of a bloomy Roquefort or the mellow nuttiness of manchego? Once you've determined your preferences, ask your cheesemonger to tell you which category of cheese you've sampled and let your research begin from there.

For further reading on cheese making, we recommend the excellent magazine *Culture: The Word on Cheese* (see Resources, page 265), a publication for cheese makers, mongers, and lovers.

RECIPE

MAKE A SIMPLE RICOTTA

Ricotta is an Italian form of fresh cheese usually made with sheep's milk. Here we've substituted fresh cow's milk and used vinegar as our acid. Experiment with using lemon juice and citric acid in place of vinegar to see how that affects the flavor.

INGREDIENTS

6 cups whole milk (unpasteurized if possible or not processed using ultra-high temperatures)

2 cups cream

3 tablespoons white vinegar

1 tablespoon kosher salt

EQUIPMENT

Strainer

Cheesecloth

4-quart pot

Makes 1 cup

DIRECTIONS

1. Line a strainer with damp cheesecloth and place over the sink.

2. In a 4-quart pot, combine the milk, cream, vinegar, and salt and bring the ingredients to a simmer (but do not let the mixture come to a boil, as this will burn your milk). After about 3 minutes, you should begin to see curds form and separate from the whey. Turn off the heat and remove the pot from the heat.

3. Pour the curds and whey into the cheesecloth, allowing the whey to pass through the cloth. Let the mixture drain for 15 minutes.

4. Remove the cheesecloth from the strainer and twist the top closed to capture the curds in one ball. Gently but firmly squeeze the curds. You don't want to remove all the whey, just the majority of it.

5. The ricotta is now ready to eat or be incorporated into a recipe and will keep refrigerated for 1 to 2 days.

RECIPE

THE GREATEST SCAPE

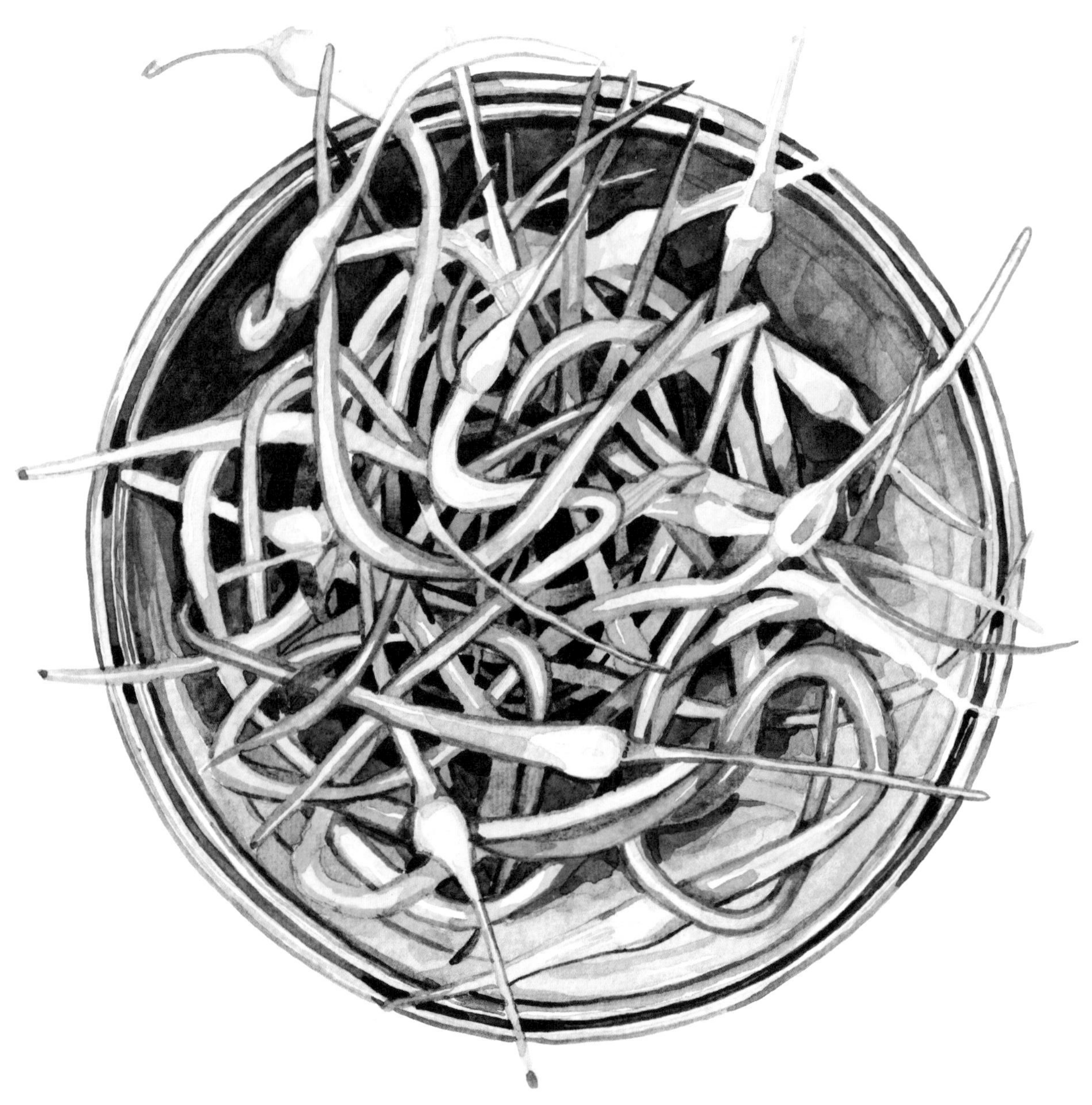

Like other methods of preserving, pickling creates an environment that is inhospitable to potentially perilous microorganisms that might find your harvest as tantalizing as you do. Pickling relies on the process of acidulation to raise the pH of your vegetable's environment to a level that is unwelcoming to microscopic interlopers, which, in addition to hot-water-bath processing, allows you to stow your harvest in room temperature cupboards until you're ready to tuck in.

Crunchy pickled cucumbers and zippy dilly beans have their place in the pickled world, but the oft-discarded garlic scape is equally deserving of space in the pantry. In the late spring and early summer, long, spindly shoots spire from garlic bulbs in a curly tangle. If left to grow, these shoots will produce a flower, taking all the energy away from the bulb and putting it toward the bloom, which produces seeds. Since it's the bulb, not the seeds, that we want to eat, farmers traditionally lop off these shoots—or scapes—so the bulb becomes more energetic and larger.

More recently, scapes are being appreciated as glorious vegetables in their own right. With a mellower flavor than garlic, scapes are spicy, bright, and aromatic. When pickled, they can be used to enhance dishes in the way pickles might in Southern cuisine—to complement potato salads, slow-braised meats, or smoky bean dishes—or in stir-fries, egg dishes, or pizzas. The long stalks also add an especially lovely, fiery, acidic heat to bloody Marys.

The acid level in this recipe is crucial. It calls for apple cider vinegar, which has a sweeter, more complex flavor than white vinegar but will color your scapes slightly. If coloration is a concern, you can substitute white vinegar; just make sure it has an acidity level of 5 percent. Also make sure you use pure kosher salt or salt that is free from iodine, which can produce a cloudy brine. As scapes can be somewhat difficult to find, this recipe is for a single pint jar's worth; if you are lucky enough to find a stash, double or triple the recipe.

INGREDIENTS

2 cups garlic scapes, washed and dried

2 cups apple cider vinegar

1 cup water

1 tablespoon kosher salt

1 dried chili

1 teaspoon coriander seeds

EQUIPMENT

1 pint-sized jar with lid

Saucepan

Funnel

Ladle

Jar lifter

Makes 1 pint

DIRECTIONS

1. Prepare the scapes by cutting off the flower and the end of each. Cut the scapes into long spears that are uniform in length. They should be able to fit inside the pint jar with ½ inch of headroom.

2. Prepare your hot water bath and sterilize your jar and lid (for instructions, see page 101). Set the jar on a towel upside down.

3. In a saucepan, bring the vinegar, water, and salt to a boil. When it has just reached a boil and the salt has dissolved, turn off the heat.

4. Quickly pack your scapes as tightly as possible in the cooled pint jar, leaving as little room for air as possible.

5. Add the dried chili and coriander seeds.

6. Ladle the hot vinegar into the sterilized jar using a funnel.

7. Wipe the rim with a damp paper towel, screw on the lid, and process the jar in boiling water for 15 minutes.

8. Remove the jar using a jar lifter and allow it to rest on a towel untouched overnight. Your sealed jar will keep in a darkened cupboard for up to 6 months. Once opened, refrigerate immediately and use within 2 weeks.

RECIPE

MAKE ELDERFLOWER CHAMPAGNE

Elderflower champagne sounds almost aristocratic, ambrosia-esque. But thanks to lowly old yeast, it's a drink anyone can create and enjoy. Yeast is a squirrely beast—one we've nurtured and pampered, pursued and prodded for thousands of years. Despite its mutable, often unpredictable ways, yeast is ubiquitous. It's between our toes. It's in our stomachs. It's sitting pretty on the tops of springtime flowers, ready to transform regular water into a fizzy, intoxicating brew.

The flavor we like best is that of elderberry flowers, which can be easily found growing along roadsides from late May to mid-June in most parts of the United States and throughout Scandinavia. You can identify the blossoms by looking at the slender green stalks, umbrella-like flower cluster, and delicate, lacy five-petal bloom—not to mention its distinctive aroma: light, creamy, and floral. Once you've found them, pick the large white flowering umbels when they are absolutely at the height of their aromatic bloom. Harvest twenty heads and carefully strip as many of the small white blossoms—sans green stems—into a large bowl using a fork or comb.

INGREDIENTS

1½ gallons water

1½ pounds granulated sugar

5 lemons

2 tablespoons apple cider vinegar

20 elderberry flower heads

Brewer's yeast (optional)

EQUIPMENT

Large pot

Tea towel

Large bowl

Sieve

Cheesecloth

Funnel

Plastic bottles

Makes approximately 1 gallon

DIRECTIONS

1. Juice and zest 4 of the lemons and cut the remaining lemon into thin slices. In a large pot, bring a gallon of water to a boil. Stir in the sugar (you can adjust the recipe for sweetness next time). Remove from the heat. Once the sugar has dissolved, add another half gallon of cold water to cool the mixture. Add the lemon juice, zest, and slices, the vinegar, and the picked flowers. Let sit for 1 hour. You are now working with wild, living yeast organisms!

2. Cover the bowl with a clean tea towel and leave in an airy, cool location to let the flavors mix and mingle for 48 hours. If the mixture hasn't started to slightly froth after this time, add a single pinch of brewer's yeast to help augment the brew's natural population.

3. Strain the mixture into a large bowl through a sieve lined with cheesecloth.

4. Use a funnel to pour it into plastic bottles. (Don't use glass bottles because this mixture ferments quickly and can explode as pressure builds.) Put the caps on the bottles, *but do not screw them on tightly,* and place in a dark, cool location for 1 to 2 weeks. Start watching the brew for bubbles. Sample the champagne for dryness as time passes and serve when it suits you. Once the brew reaches optimum flavor for your palate, screw the tops on tightly and place in the fridge. The coolness will stop fermentation and the delicious brew will keep refrigerated for 2 to 3 weeks.

SPRING

HOME & SELF-RELIANCE

SPRING

PREPARE YOUR HOME FOR THE SEASON

In spring, the outdoors can once again be welcomed indoors and the indoors can be moved outside. Open your windows to get a burst of fresh air inside your home, and let your houseplants bask in outdoor sunlight. Celebrate the change in seasons by participating in the age-old tradition of spring-cleaning, tidying, and preparing your home for the busy growing season to come.

- ☐ **Make a batch of household cleaners to use throughout the year.**
- ☐ **Mend fences before the summer season commences.**
- ☐ **Move tropical household plants outdoors when the weather turns fair.**
- ☐ **Hang birdhouses outdoors.**
- ☐ **Remove any additional insulated window treatments to allow fresh air to circulate.**
- ☐ **Organize and clean up any bulbs stored away for winter.**
- ☐ **Scout for early appearing weeds, such as field pennycress, in pasture and garden beds.**
- ☐ **Clean out the chicken coop and add manure to the compost.**
- ☐ **Turn livestock back onto pasture.**
- ☐ **Groom your animals outdoors to give them lustrous, thinner summer coats.**
- ☐ **Prepare nest boxes for chickens to get ready for increased laying.**
- ☐ **Pickle first-of-the-season asparagus and ramps for year-round use.**
- ☐ **Feed houseplants their first dose of fertilizer.**
- ☐ **Start cuttings of houseplants to double your plants by fall.**
- ☐ **Give chickens access to bare ground so they can take dust baths to ward off mites.**
- ☐ **Use fresh, seasonal milk to make homemade cheese and butter (for a primer on cheese making, see page 36).**
- ☐ **Check your house eaves for signs of hornets' nests and knock them down early, before they grow.**
- ☐ **Mow areas of tall grass so chickens can eat the new tender shoots.**
- ☐ **Begin the vigil for insects; make sure all food is properly stored.**
- ☐ **Take an inventory of immediate predators in the area and make a plan to deal with foxes, coyotes, raccoons, or other unwelcome guests.**

KNOWLEDGE

DYES IN THE WILD

Browse through the racks at any clothing boutique and you'll see a kaleidoscope of colors: neon brights, metallic shimmers, hyper-saturated blacks—colors that couldn't be found in clothing until very recently. Though the evidence of the first dyes used on textiles dates back over five thousand years, it has only been since the nineteenth century that synthetic dyes have been developed—and extraordinary colors like neon hues even more recently than that. Before the nineteenth century, specialized craftsmen and -women relied on roots, shells, stems, flowers, leaves, and even eggs to make high-chroma pigments like royal or Tyrian purple (made from snail secretions), rich scarlet (made from the intact, granular eggs of the kermes insect), or crimson carmine (made from the crushed shells of the cochineal bug).

Today, most clothing and textiles that you'll find on the market have been dyed using one of a few methods, depending on the fiber used to make the cloth: direct dyeing, vat dyeing, sulphur dyeing, or reactive dyeing. With fiber-reactive dyeing—one of the most popular methods—synthetic chemicals, salt, and large amounts of water are used to adhere dye to cloth. Though this process produces gorgeous, rich hues, it carries with it some cautionary consequences. The EPA estimates that between five and thirty-five gallons of water are used to create each pound of fabric. In that water, about 80 percent of the dye particles adhere to the fibers of the cloth and the remaining 20 percent are rinsed out of the cloth and sent down our drains, releasing chemicals like mercury, lead, chromium, and benzene into our waterways and farmland. Keep in mind, the dye particles that do adhere to the cloth impart the same chemicals to the clothing that touches your skin.

The Natural Alternative

Thankfully, many clothing companies and artisans are embracing the dyeing methods that were used for centuries before the advent of synthetics in the 1850s. Beginning with William Morris and the arts and crafts movement and continuing through to contemporary artists and artisans, natural dyeing has been making a steady comeback since its downfall during the industrial revolution.

The art of natural dyeing is a bit like alchemy; when fiber matter, plant matter, and water are combined, a new substance emerges. Though much research has gone into how this works, it can still seem a bit like magic even to the most experienced technician.

The basic process of natural dyeing uses plant or animal matter to stain a water bath. If necessary, a mordant—a water-soluble metallic salt like copper, tin or iron, table salt, alum, or vinegar—is incorporated into the dye bath to fix the dye to the fiber. The cloth is then simmered, immersed, or left in the sun to soak in the solution before being rinsed clean. The particular type of mordant, the plant matter, and the fiber will interact to create a unique color, so testing of each combination is recommended in order to get the exact hue you're after—it's in the blend where the magic happens, after all.

To Make Natural Dyes

To make a dye solution using plants (see sidebar), you'll need to chop up the plant matter and simmer it with twice the amount of water as plant matter for one hour. Prepare your fabric (cotton, wool, or silk only) by washing it first and then soaking it in a bucket or large pot in either salt, for berry dyes (1 part salt to 8 parts water), or vinegar, for plant dyes (1 part vinegar to 4 parts water), for one hour. Experiment with other mordants to reveal a different color from the plant matter. Remove your fabric from the soaking water, wring out the excess water, and place the fabric and the prepared dye in a large metal pot (one that won't be used for cooking) for several hours or overnight, stirring frequently. In the morning, rise with warm water until the water runs clear. Let dry, and it'll be ready to wear.

NOW IN TECHNICOLOR

The gorgeous spectrum of colors in the environment around us can be harnessed to create a palette of natural dyes. Below are suggestions for creating colors.

FOR RED

Beets, madder (root), rosehips, hibiscus (flower), sycamore (bark)

FOR ORANGE

Barberry (any part), bloodroot (root), carrots (root), onions (skin), pomegranates (skin)

FOR YELLOW

Tansy (tops), saffron (stigmas), Queen Anne's lace, goldenrod (flowers), crocus (flowers)

FOR GREEN

Lilacs (flowers), grass, nettles, spinach, yarrow (flowers)

FOR BLUE TO PURPLE

Red cabbage, mulberries, blueberries, woad (leaves), indigofera (leaves)

FOR PINK

Strawberries (fruit, not leaves), cherries (fruit not stem), camellias (petals), roses (petals), lavender (petals)

FOR BROWN

Acorns (whole, boiled), coffee grounds, tea bags, walnuts (husk), goldenrod (shoots)

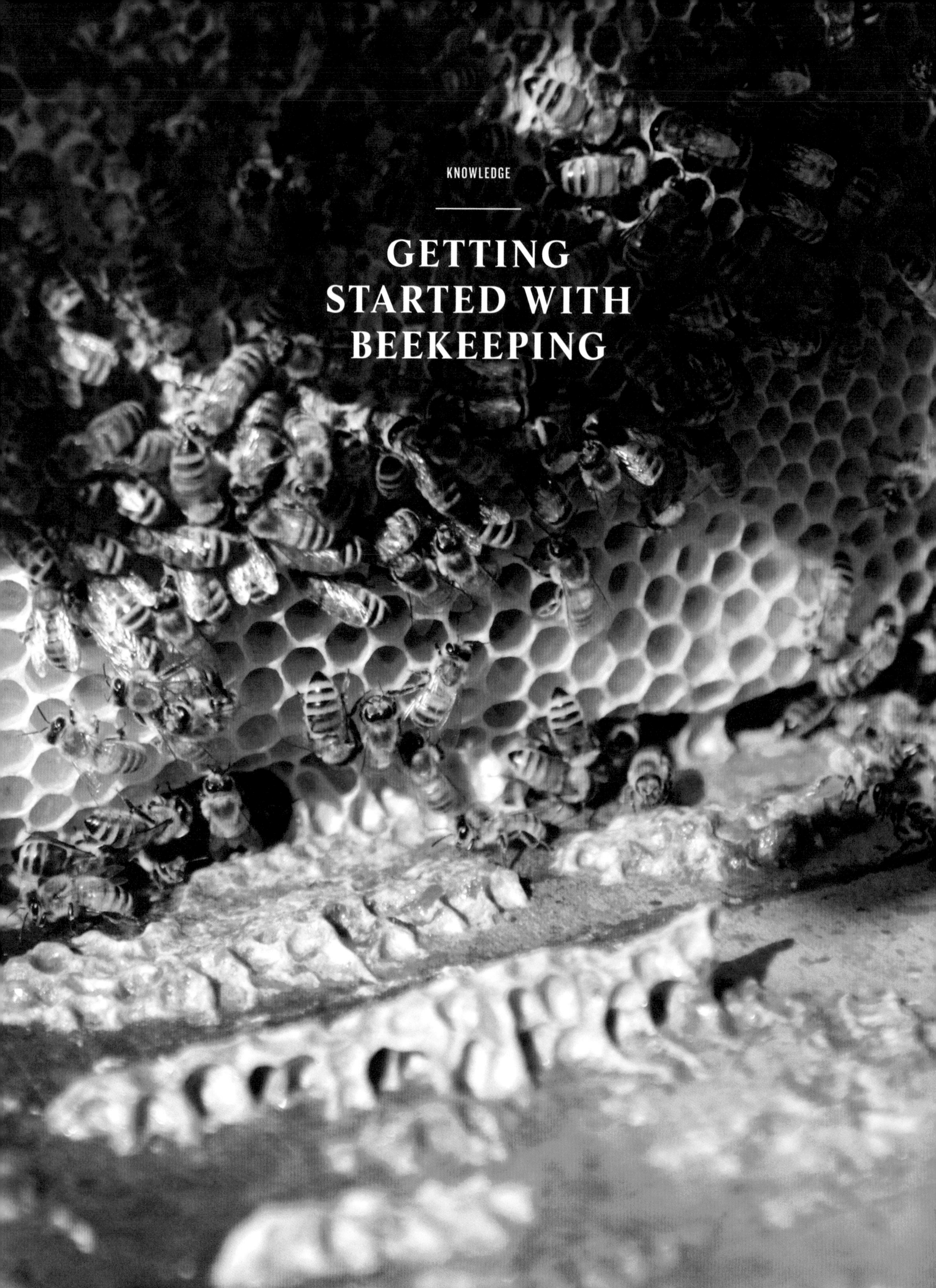

GETTING STARTED WITH BEEKEEPING

Imagine golden honey dripping from a slice of hot buttered toast or a teaspoon of honey sweetening your morning cup of tea and the benefits of keeping a hive seem obvious—almost as obvious as the pointed, stinging reason not to. Beekeeping can be a glorious, productive hobby for the unintimidated. Aside from the benefit of gaining insight into Mother Nature's intricate patterns, fresh honey and beeswax for candles, lip balms, and salves await if you're feeling bold.

Bees work together in an organized system called a colony to ensure the propagation of their species. The structure the colony inhabits is called a hive, and a hive can be naturally occurring or man-made. Each colony is ruled by a queen bee, who is the sole egg layer, and inhabited by thousands of female, infertile worker bees and a limited number of male drone bees. The queen bee is the eldest of the colony and will spend her entire life laying eggs. The worker bees are responsible for building a honeycomb to protect and house the eggs, collecting pollen and water from blossoms that are transformed into fat stores for the winter months (this becomes what we know as honey) and regulating the internal temperature of the hive. The drone bees do not leave the hive, but rather eat the honey stores and wait for the right time to mate with the queen bee, before they meet their untimely end.

Eloise Augustyn, owner and head chef of Portland, Oregon's Sweedeedee, is an enthusiastic beekeeper. Augustyn raises her own hive in the urban limits of Portland, and she advises you take the following steps to begin your journey into beekeeping.

START EARLY. Start in the winter. Study and prepare for the spring season ahead. Research and select the style of hive you want. Build or purchase the hive by early spring.

PLACE YOUR HIVE IN ITS NEW HOME. Once the hive is in hand, think carefully about the placement of your hive. Placement is very important; you cannot move the hive once the bees arrive. Once the hive is active, it can only be moved either as little as three feet or a distance of at least two miles or more. Rooftops are just as enticing real estate as gardens are for bees. Make sure the hive is protected from harsh weather, sun, wind, and rain. Morning sun is good for the bees, but protection from the strong afternoon heat in the summer months is essential. Also consider the flight path of the bees; don't place the entrance of the hive facing a pathway or picnic area.

COLLECT YOUR EQUIPMENT. It is important to wear protective clothing when working with bees. You will get bee stings as a beekeeper, so minimize them by wearing beekeeping gloves (or leather gloves) and a bee veil or jacket when working with bees. You'll also need a bee box and a hive tool, as well as your own bee book library.

SOURCE YOUR BEES. Decide how you would like to begin your colony. Ordering bees from a beekeeping supply shop is best done between April and late June.

WORK WITH THE BEES. Working with bees will remind you how important it is to move in life with care and intention; approach the task with openness and flexibility. You may go into your hive with a plan, but always be attentive to the energy that the bees give off, reading each situation and adjusting whenever necessary to understand all the ways the bees communicate. (For further reading on how to work with bees, see Resources, page 265.)

HARVEST HONEY. You will know when it's time to harvest the honey by checking the honeycomb. If there is a wax cap on about 80 percent of the honeycomb, it is time to harvest. The type of equipment you will need depends on the type of hive you have. Household items like the beater from an electric mixer can be used to crush the cells of the honeycomb and strain out the honey. Or a honey extractor tool can be purchased. The extractor will leave the cells intact; the crush and strain method will not. If using the crush and strain method, heat the remaining crushed cells and then allow the mixture to cool. The beeswax will rise to the top and the honey will sink to the bottom. Scrape off the beeswax and use it in salves or candles.

CARE FOR THE HIVE. Get to know the rhythm of your hive. Harvest during the spring and summer, but be sure your bees have their winter stores full before cold weather hits.

HOW TO WEAVE ON A FRAME LOOM

Different types of looms can be found around the world, from the complex Jacquard to the more humble back-strap. Each type of loom has its own style and limitations, but the basic function of weaving remains as it has for centuries: one thread goes over and one goes under to make a grid system. The grid system uses two perpendicular sets of threads; the vertical threads are called the warp, and the horizontal threads are called the weft.

You can create a simple frame loom with minimal tools, many of which you may already have at home. Los Angeles–based artist Christy Matson taught us to make a frame loom by using a picture frame with the back removed. This method makes a weaving the same size as the frame that you've chosen. When you select the warp threads, make sure they are sturdy. When looking at raw weft material, be creative—yarn of different weights or wool roving will create different effects on the finished piece. The combination of yarns you choose will create your design.

WHAT YOU'LL NEED

1 small to medium-sized picture frame with the back and glass removed

Thick wool yarn for warp material

A variety of yarn for weft material

Wooden ruler

Dinner fork or comb

DIRECTIONS

1. Warp the loom by tying a knot at the bottom edge on the left-hand side of the picture frame with your wool warp yarn. Loop the yarn continuously between the top and bottom of the picture frame, moving from left to right. About eight threads per inch is a good spacing to aim for.

2. Cut about a yard of weft yarn; fold it in half. Place the center of the yarn at the bottom left-hand side of the warp with one side above and one side below the first warp yarn. Twist the yarn once to enclose the first warp. Keeping the yarn taut, enclose the second warp yarn by repeating the single twist. Repeat until you have created a row. Finish with an overhand knot. The warps should be evenly spaced and not touching. Do the same thing at the top edge.

3. Insert the ruler (your "shed stick") into the warp yarn. Pass it over and under groups of two warp yarns.

4. Turn the ruler on its side to create an opening. Insert a weft yarn into the opening on either the left or right side of the ruler.

5. Rotate the ruler so that it is flat and push one weft yarn to the top of the weaving, the other to the bottom. Use your fingers, a dinner fork, or a comb to pack the thread down. Remove the ruler and reinsert it with the opposite pairs of warp yarns on top and bottom of the stick and continue weaving.

6. When you can no longer insert the ruler into the warp yarns, pass the weft yarn through the warp with your fingers or thread it onto a large needle to finish the weaving.

7. To remove the weaving from the frame, cut along the outer top and bottom edges of the frame. The knotted edge will prevent your weaving from unraveling.

SPRING

BEAUTY & HEALING

KNOWLEDGE

A SEASONAL APOTHECARY

When the days grow longer, even a few extra minutes of sunlight can feel like a gift. The heaviness of winter starts to fade away and you, like a little green plant shoot, can spring forth and welcome the season of awakening and growth. Of course, spring isn't all butterflies and flower petals. The blossoms we crave all winter long bring with them pollen and other allergens that can make this time of year a teary-eyed season for some. To help fend off runny noses, fight winter's lethargy, and jump-start our bodies back into action, here are the wild ingredients to reach for when you need a boost in spring. For directions on how to use the herbs, see below.

HERBS TO DETOX

Dandelion
An anti-inflammatory, cleanser, and diuretic. Use as a culinary herb, food, or tea.

Garlic
A potent antibacterial that aids in eliminating infection. Use as a culinary herb or oil.

HERBS TO RESTORE VITALITY

Holy Basil
Renews and balances energy and promotes long life. Use as a tincture.

HERBS TO HOLISTICALLY CLEANSE AND BRIGHTEN

Lemon Balm
Calms and relaxes the nervous system. Aids in heartache and transition. Use as a tea or tincture.

Peppermint
An invigorating pick-me-up to stimulate the body and mind. Use as a tea, culinary herb, or oil.

Red Clover
Helps tone lymphatic congestion and can act as a "blood purifier." Use as an infusion with honey.

Saint-John's-Wort
Superior antidepressant, antiviral, and aid for seasonal changes. Use as a tea, tincture, or salve.

HERBS TO COMBAT ALLERGIES

Mullein
For chest congestion, bronchial stress, and allergies. Use as a tea or salve.

Nettles
High in vitamins A, C, and D, it helps soothe allergies and hay fever. Use as a tea.

Yarrow
Helpful for colds, flu, or allergies. Tones the circulatory system. Use as a tea or tincture.

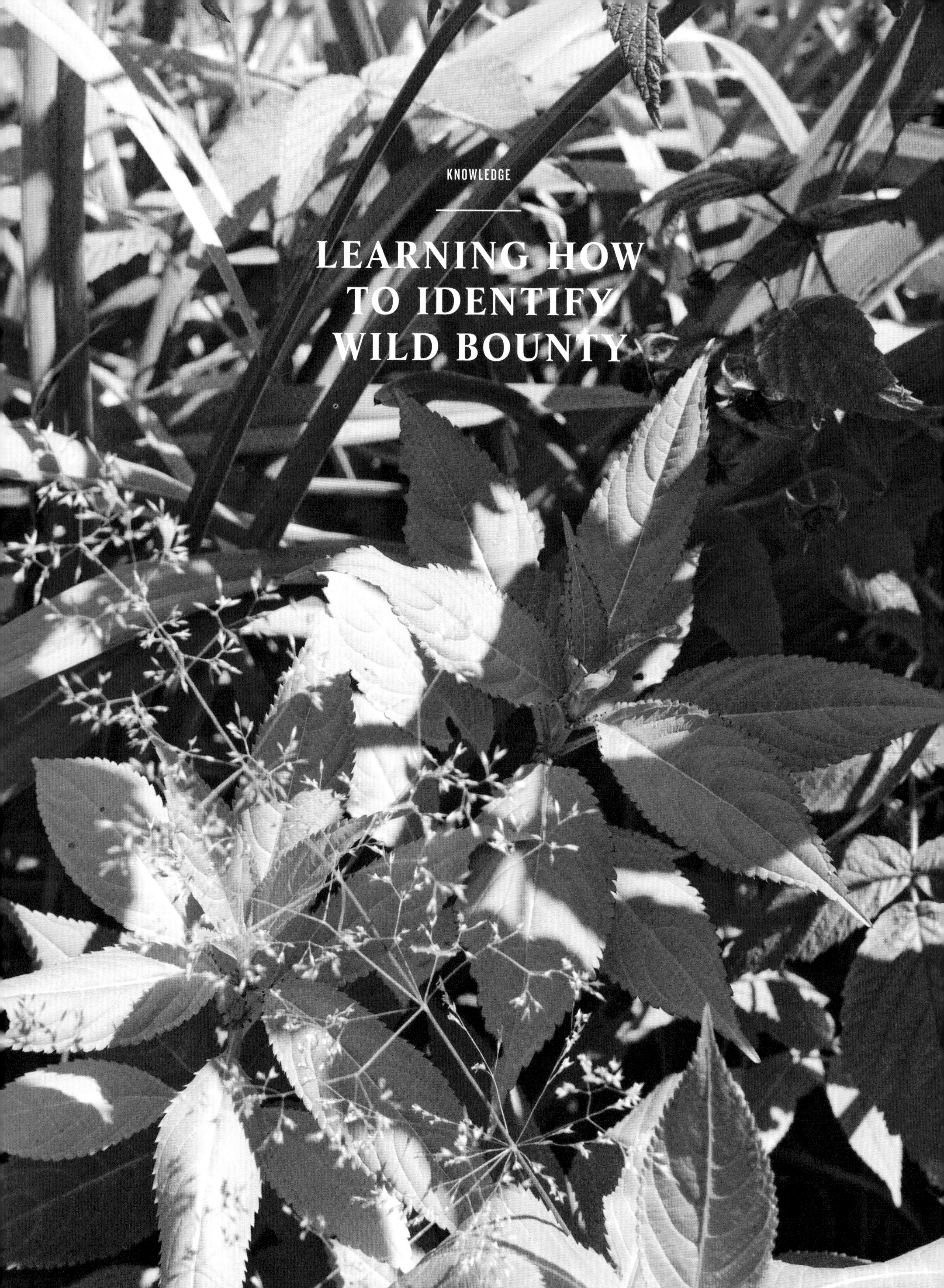

KNOWLEDGE

LEARNING HOW TO IDENTIFY WILD BOUNTY

The original definition of wild crafting is quite simple: harvesting from nature. Recently, the term has come to mean different things, but we think of it as harvesting plants and putting them to good use—whether it's making beauty treatments, medicinal treatments, or food. In your everyday encounters, you likely pass by vital and healing plants that many consider weeds. Pay a bit of attention to your surroundings, do some research, and you'll begin to see the beauty and benefit of the world around you. Here are some guidelines to ensure that you're respecting nature while taking part in its magic.

LEARN YOUR HABITAT. Get to know your biome and habitat. Save yourself from an endless search for cattails if you happen to live in an arid region. Learn about where you live. Plantnative.org is a great resource to find out what grows in your habitat.

KNOW YOUR POISON. Observe the power of nature. Just as there are benefits to be gleaned from our wild world, there are also plants that are dangerous to us if ingested or applied to our skin. Know the common harmful plants that grow in your region and where they frequently lurk. Many will be listed for you in your native plant list. For questions about specific plants, check with the Centers for Disease Control and Prevention (CDC).

USE YOUR LIBRARY SKILLS. Always bring an illustrated guidebook with you when foraging. Use the guide to double-check before you pick something.

SPEAK LATIN. Plants travel under many names, and their common name is by far the least reliable. When looking to take something found in the wild into your body in any way, make sure you have identified the plant by its correct binomial.

KNOW YOUR PARTS. Not all parts of a plant function in the same way. In a single plant, the roots, leaves, and flowers may all serve a special use. Make sure you know what part of the plant you will need to serve your purpose before removing it from the wild.

HARVEST RESPONSIBLY. Plants and flowers may seem like they grow in abundance in the wild, but in truth these resources are part of a larger ecosystem that we should not disturb. Take from multiple plants and take only what you truly need for the task at hand. Selective reseeding may help to lessen your impact on the area.

BE PREPARED TO CARRY WHAT YOU COLLECT. When traveling out in the hinterland, bear in mind that whatever you harvest you will have to carry back home with as little damage as possible. Choose a shallow basket for carrying your bounty to protect the delicate leaves and roots while still allowing air to pass through them.

OUR MOST SOUGHT-AFTER FINDS

Depending on where you live and what your personal interest is, you will find the world around you endlessly generative. Look for ingredients that speak to you the most. For us, the ingredients listed below are some of our most personally loved.

BEACH ROSE (*Rosa rugosa*)

A coastal rose that blooms near the sea in New England and on the West Coast, the Rosa rugosa's blooms produce a pungent floral fragrance (see how to make perfume on page 131) and are highly aromatic when dried. The fruit itself can be used to make marmalade or jelly.

DANDELION (*Taraxacum officinale*)

A foe of the green lawn, dandelions grow in abundance in the spring. Harvest the leaves to sauté as vitamin-rich food or use the root to make a powerful tincture for liver health.

PLANTAIN (*Plantago major*)

Commonly seen peeking through sidewalks, plantain can even be foraged in urban environments. Harvest the leaves to create a medicinal oil or further process them into a salve to soothe irritated skin.

RED CLOVER (*Trifolium pratense*)

Red clover is a friend to the honeybee and herbalist alike. Rich in vitamins C and B, the blossoms can be eaten raw in salads or as a garnish for soups. Combine the flowers and leaves and steep in hot water for a nutrient-rich tea.

DIY

MAKE AN HERBAL TINCTURE

Tinctures are liquid extracts meant for oral use, and they're an easy way to impart the healing essence of seasonal herbs, plants, and flowers year-round. The alcohol used in this recipe will extract the precious oils, resins, and alkaloids from whichever plants you choose. Use only the leaves and flowers of freshly cut plants, and in the interest of preservation, pick only what you need.

Though easy to make, it is important to be mindful of how you store a tincture. Always remember to carefully label and date your creation and keep it in a dark drawer or cupboard where it will be protected from damage and aging from sunlight. With proper conditions in place, tinctures should last for up to one year.

NOTE: It is always best to consult a health-care practitioner before beginning any new health regimen.

Recommended Tinctures

For deep sleep, use 4 parts valerian root to 1 part lavender.

For headaches, use 2 parts peppermint to 1 part chamomile.

For mild depression, use 2 parts Saint-John's-wort flower to 1 part lemon balm leaves.

INGREDIENTS

5 cups fresh plant matter, such as peppermint, lavender, or valerian root

2 cups 100-proof alcohol (brandy or vodka is recommended; or apple cider vinegar may be used if you cannot tolerate alcohol)

EQUIPMENT

One 16-ounce Mason jar with lid

Four 4-ounce amber glass bottles with droppers

Dish towel

Wooden spoon

Cheesecloth

Glass mixing bowl

4-cup glass measuring cup

Adhesive labels

DIRECTIONS

1. Sterilize your Mason jar and amber glass bottles by placing the jars and lids in boiling water for 10 to 15 minutes. Allow the jars and lids to cool upside down on a clean, dry dish towel.

2. Finely chop the plant matter and place it in the Mason jar, leaving 2 inches of space at the top. Discard leftover, unusable plant matter.

3. Fill the Mason jar with the alcohol, leaving 1 inch of space at the top.

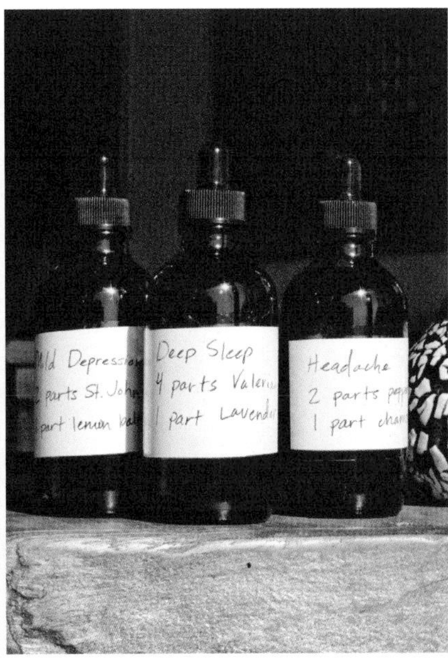

4. Stir the mixture with a wooden spoon in a clockwise motion vigorously enough so that a small vortex forms in the middle.

5. Seal the mixture and store in a dark place for 2 to 6 weeks; shake the jar daily.

6. Set a piece of cheesecloth over a glass mixing bowl and strain the mixture through the cheesecloth. When all the herbs are gathered in the cheesecloth, gently squeeze the cloth to release any excess liquid still in the herbs. Discard the herbs and clean the cheesecloth for reuse. Using the measuring cup, dispense the tincture into the amber glass bottles, one cup per bottle.

7. Label and date your tincture and store in a dark cupboard or drawer. Take the tincture diluted in tea, juice, or water, or administer directly on the tongue—20 to 30 drops daily as needed.

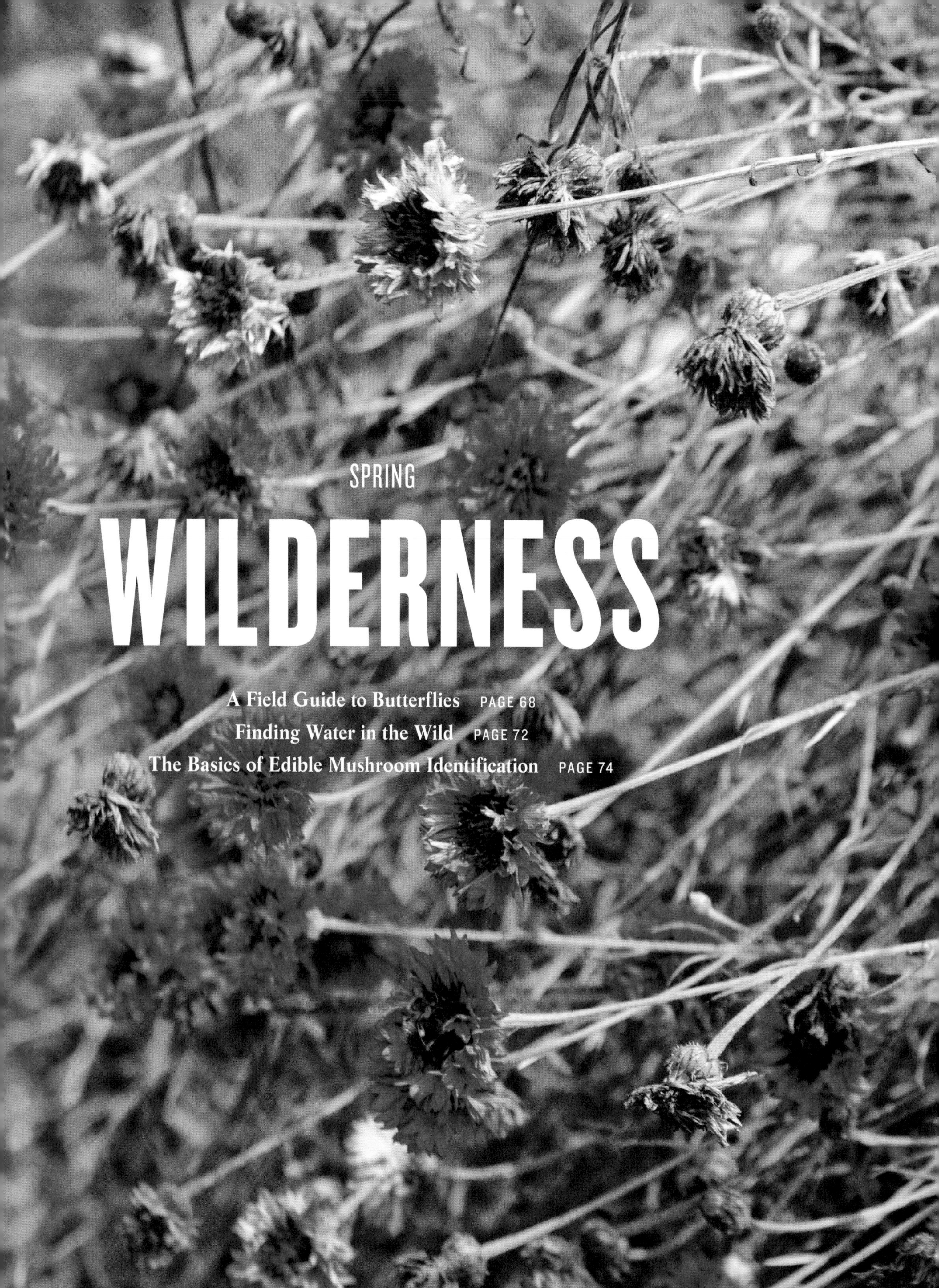

SPRING

WILDERNESS

KNOWLEDGE

A FIELD GUIDE TO BUTTERFLIES

No matter the size of your garden, from a big backyard to a tiny city window box, there's a very simple recipe for attracting butterflies: plant flowers—and lots of them. Butterflies crave nectar and pollen-rich flowers, so choose those with the highest yield to ensure that butterflies appear. Some of our easy-to-grow favorites include the butterfly bush (*Buddleia*), catmint (*Nepeta*), false indigo (*Baptisia*), Helen's flower (*Helenium*), lilac (*Syringa*), purple coneflower (*Echinacea*), sea holly (*Eryngium*), and zinnia (*Zinnia*). Plants with a tube-shaped or tubular flower, like crowd-pleasing lavender (*Lavendula*) and mint (*Mentha*), are also stars.

Once your flowers are in bloom, the butterflies will be sure to follow. Here are some easy tricks to identifying some of our favorites from across the world. Happy hunting!

MIDWEST UNITED STATES

Coral Hairstreak

HABITAT: Overgrown fields, bushes, forests, and woodlands

IDENTIFICATION TIPS: An uncommon butterfly with a delicate grayish-brown coloring and a prominent row of coral spots along its hind wing.

FAVORITE FLOWER: Butterfly milkweed

Purplish Copper

HABITAT: Just about everywhere from meadows and marshes to cities

IDENTIFICATION TIPS: All butterflies are beautiful, but the purplish copper is a standout with its almost iridescent purple-pink wings. The hind wings of the male also have a scalloped pale orange trim.

FAVORITE FLOWER: Purplish copper

NORTHWEST UNITED STATES

Lorquin's Admiral

HABITAT: Loves two locales: the riverside and the edge of a forest or an orchard

IDENTIFICATION TIPS: The "admiral" has a distinct white band that crosses along both wings, and a spot of orange on the forewings, to brighten up the palette.

FAVORITE FLOWER: The flowers of the weeping willow or the poplar tree

Pale Swallowtail

HABITAT: Throughout much of the western United States near water and at higher altitudes

IDENTIFICATION TIPS: This common butterfly has creamy white wings with black horizontal stripes.

FAVORITE FLOWER: The beautiful shrub *Ceanothus*, or California lilac

MOUNTAIN WEST UNITED STATES AND LOWER CANADA

Anicia Checkerspot

HABITAT: Mountain ridges along forest edges, in orchards, and on clearings

IDENTIFICATION TIPS: While this butterfly is common, it's always a stunning sight. A fiery range of colors—dark reds, burnt oranges, and sooty black—makes up its namesake checkerboard pattern.

FAVORITE FLOWER: Yerba santa

Woodland Skipper

HABITAT: Swamps, bogs, and marshes, along with forests and woodlands

IDENTIFICATION TIPS: With its dark brown and tan coloring, this butterfly looks like the wood of its habitat. It is also hairy and mothlike, having the ability to hold its wings simultaneously flat.

FAVORITE FLOWER: Native grasses such as the blue wild rye

SOUTHWEST UNITED STATES

Buckeye

HABITAT: Anywhere sunny, from gardens to parks and roadsides

IDENTIFICATION TIPS: Take one look at this butterfly and you'll know why it's called the buckeye. This is the iconic butterfly look, with large eyespots in the corners of its wings, ranging in color from brown to faded reds.

FAVORITE FLOWER: Snapdragon

Question Mark

HABITAT: Across North America but predominant in the Southwest; associated with moist, wooded areas

IDENTIFICATION TIPS: The question mark is an incredible looking butterfly. It's often mistaken for a dried leaf and described as cryptic with its blended colors.

FAVORITE FLOWER: Milkweed

SOUTH AND SOUTHEASTERN UNITED STATES

Gulf Fritillary

HABITAT: Scattered throughout the southern United States in open sunny areas; a common garden visitor

IDENTIFICATION TIPS: This hard-to-miss bright orange butterfly has elongated wings with black-encircled white dots on the edges.

FAVORITE FLOWER: Passion vines

Sleepy Orange

HABITAT: Abundant at the edges of woods, valleys, and damp areas

IDENTIFICATION TIPS: Despite its name, the sleepy orange moves rapidly once in flight. If you can, take stock of its orange coloring and small black spot on the forewing. In the winter, the underside of the hind wing is red or brown. In summer, it's an eye-catching orange to yellow.

FAVORITE FLOWER: Beggar tick

EUROPE

Adonis Blue

HABITAT: Grasslands (The number of these butterflies has been in decline, although due to conservationists' efforts, they are starting to make a comeback.)

IDENTIFICATION TIPS: Males can boast sky-blue wings, while females have a dusty, eye-catching brown coloring. Both have a white border with dark lines, which extend across into the wings' fringe.

FAVORITE FLOWER: Horseshoe vetch

Orange Tip

HABITAT: Rivers, damp grasslands, gardens with bodies of water

IDENTIFICATION TIPS: Bright orange tinges the tips of the male's wings, while females feature black wing tips. It is far easier to catch site of the males as they are often on the hunt for a mate.

FAVORITE FLOWER: Cuckoo flower

SOUTHEAST ASIA

Common Archduke

HABITAT: Forest edges, areas of dense foliage

IDENTIFICATION TIPS: If you catch sight of an "archduke," you'll surely never forget it—the male's metallic shimmer along the wings' edge is impressive. Females, while less iridescent, also offer an exciting palette, with a base of dark brown and a muted, colorful pattern atop.

FAVORITE FLOWER: Cuckoo flower

Redspot Sawtooth

HABITAT: Riverbanks, roadsides, and forest edges

IDENTIFICATION TIPS: This butterfly features a splash of yellow, like a rising sun, at the center of its overly large black and white wings.

FAVORITE FLOWER: Indian heliotrope

SKILL

FINDING WATER IN THE WILD

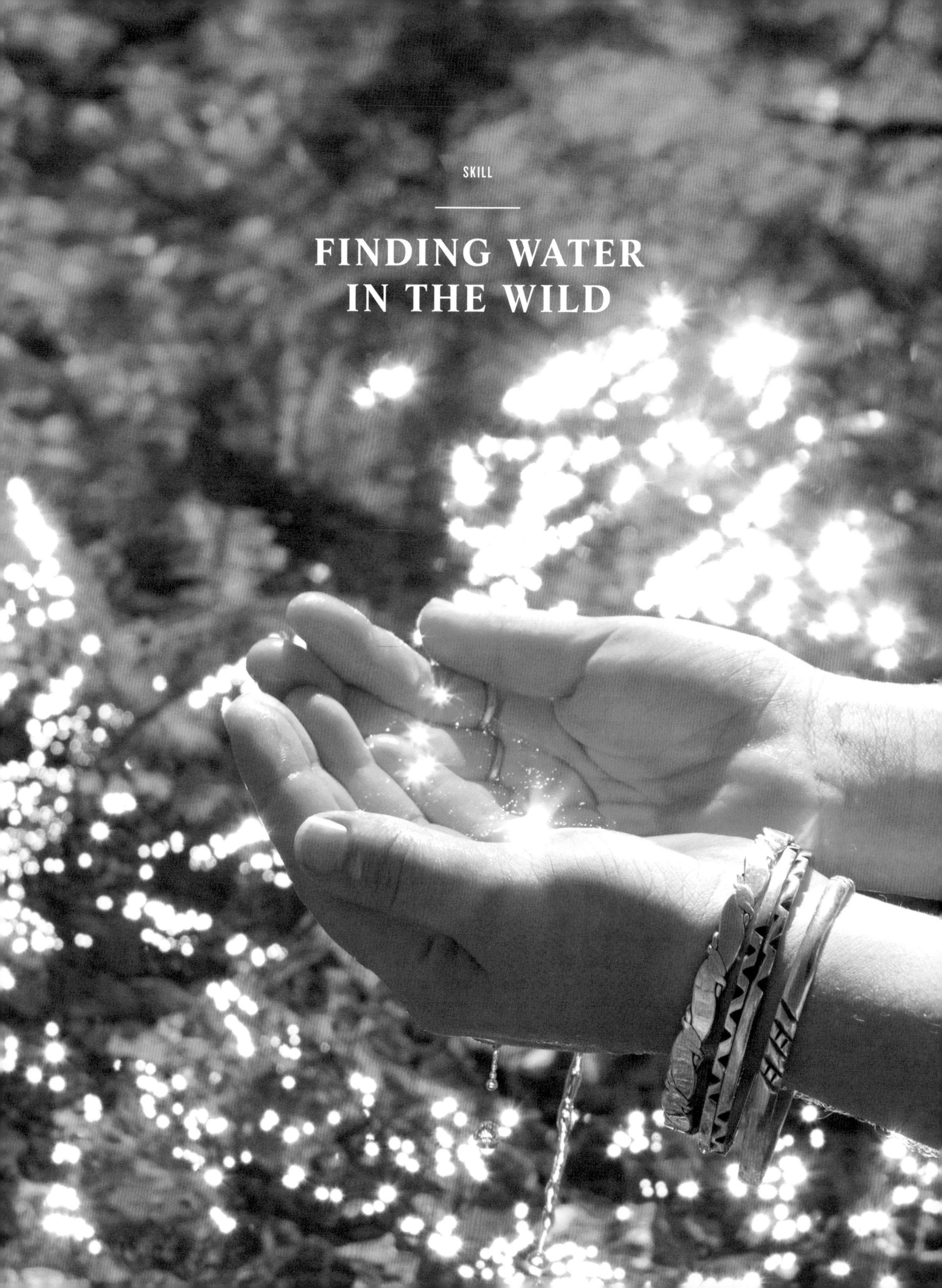

Every hiker, wild crafter, or camper should know the basics of finding and purifying water.

Getting turned around in the wild or losing a canteen can happen to anyone. Without water, your body begins to decline fairly rapidly. After an hour, you might start feeling the onset of a headache. After a day without water, a deep confusion and lethargy could set in, making it that much harder to find your way out of the predicament.

The first thing to know is that most water sources in the wild are contaminated. Not just with toxic chemicals but with parasites and dangerous bacteria, too. Common strains such as giardiasis can cause several days of extreme discomfort while others, like typhoid, can prove fatal fast. Here's what to look for when you're on the search for water.

Locate a Water Source

- **LOOK AROUND.** Is the area rich with vegetation? If so, odds are that you aren't too far away from a water source.
- **LOOK CLOSELY.** Natural formations like crevices appear where water may have collected during a recent rainstorm.
- **LOOK UP.** Birds and insects often stay close to water sources.
- **LOOK DOWN.** Notice if the ground nearby is damp. If so, dig a hole that is just about one foot deep. If you're lucky, you'll find the hole filling with muddy water. Strain this through the cloth of your T-shirt and drink it. Doing so is risky (those nasty microbes again), but just a little water can help you maintain clarity for a few key hours.

Make a Filter

Once you've located a water source, you'll want to purify the water as best you can. If you happen to have a match and pot, boil the water until it's rolling. If you're not so lucky to have the equipment to boil water, here are some simple instructions for filtering water in the wild.

- **FIND A CONTAINER.** Any container. Punch holes in the bottom. If you don't have a container, make a cone from the bark of a tree.
- **MAKE A FILTER.** Pebbles or your T-shirt will suffice.
- **ADD A LAYER OF GRAVEL.** The main purpose of the gravel layer is to strengthen the filter material, ensuring that a minimal amount of sand mixes with the water.
- **POUR THE WATER SOURCE THROUGH YOUR IMPROVISED FILTER.** This filter is rudimentary and may not be able to filter out all of the dangerous elements. Your goal should be to get just enough water into your body to stay coherent, have energy, and find your way out of the woods. Good luck!

SKILL

THE BASICS OF EDIBLE MUSHROOM IDENTIFICATION

Take a walk through the woods and most likely you'll stumble upon a mushroom or two. But how do you know if those wonders are poisonous mushrooms or if they might just be the perfect addition to your dinner plate? Mushroom identification is a true art, but a layperson can easily learn to recognize their edible favorites.

While there are hundreds of edible mushroom varieties, the easiest to identify are the "foolproof four." These mushrooms, so named by well-known mycophile David Arora, are not only delicious, they also have very few poisonous look-alikes and highly identifiable characteristics, which make them easy targets for first-time mushroom hunters.

Knowing the four primary structural elements will make it far easier for you to tell the difference between an edible delight and a poisonous 'shroom.

- **CAP**: the umbrella-shaped "hat" atop the stalk
- **STALK**: the base of the mushroom
- **GILLS, TUBES, SPINES, AND RIDGES**: what lives on the underside of the cap and releases spores
- **MYCELIUM**: roots that push the mushroom up for spore dispersal and are the avenues through which the mushroom receives nourishment

A word of caution: Before you eat any mushroom, check and double-check the mushroom's identification. If you're not 100 percent sure, err on the side of caution and don't consume it.

Chanterelles

Considered a culinary delicacy since the 1700s because of their bright, peppery flavor, chanterelles are made for the starring role in any dish.

WHERE TO FIND THEM: At the base of a tree or intertwined in a plant's roots

COLORING: Bright yellow, almost golden

CAP: Convex or a funnel with turned-up edges

STALK: Bare with no bulb around the base

GILLS: Primitive; they look as though they have melted

SMELL: Mildly of fruit, specifically like apricot

Morels

Morels are an indicator of spring, popping up in early to mid-April. With their delicate flavor, the mushrooms are perfect partners for pastas.

WHERE TO FIND THEM: In early spring, take a look around the edge of a forest or wooded area. If you can, head straight for an elm, apple, or ash tree—dead or alive—as morels love to set up camp beneath these varieties.

COLORING: Light to darker shades of brown

CAP: Conical shaped, covered in wavy ridges or pits. The cap is hollow inside.

STALK: The cap is fully or mostly attached to the stalk.

GILLS: None

SMELL: Earthy

Giant Puffball

Puffballs have a texture akin to that of tofu, making them a terrific meat substitute. They have a mild, pleasant taste and should be cooked before eating.

WHERE TO FIND THEM: Unlike the other five, this mushroom grows alone or with several others in open pastures and on lawns from May to October.

COLORING: Sculptured or scaled white to tarnished-white exterior and a smooth marshmallow interior texture. The flesh must be firm and white throughout. Any darker shades such as purple or brown means they are inedible. The flesh must be undifferentiated with no trace of gills.

CAP: White with white to light brown textured marks all over

STALK: Absent

GILLS: Absent

SMELL: A strong, unpleasant odor when young and a mild fishlike odor when more mature

Chicken of the Woods

This mushroom's claim to fame is just what you think. It tastes like chicken! Use it when recipes call for poultry.

WHERE TO FIND THEM: Stacked on trees or in stumps from spring until autumn

COLORING: Yellow to orange with an edge or lining that is a brighter shade

CAP: Overlapping, flat, fan shaped

STALK: None

GILLS: None

SMELL: Very mild scent

For those looking to learn more about the craft of mushroom identification, here are our favorite resources:

- The incredible *Mushrooms Demystified* by David Arora, which offers descriptions of more than two thousand species of mushroom.
- The Audubon Society's mushroom identification app for use when you're on the hunt.
- Classes. Most cities play host to a mycological society that can teach you to be a true mycophile.

Summer

SUMMER IS THE SEASON OF NATURAL MAGIC,

filled with the secret codes of fireflies and the hair-raising surprise of flash storms. The sunny days seem endless with possibility and the long nights are destined for adventure. As the writer Charles Bowden said, "Summertime is always the best of what might be." And for that, it is the season we wait for all year long.

Whether you sweat it out in the city or head to the country to dodge the heat, take time to revel in the season's bounty and blissfully prolonged sunlight. If you're in the northeastern part of the United States, enjoy the rituals of a New England summer: cold coastal-water dips in the ocean and late-night clambakes and forkfuls of blueberry pie. The forests are buzzing this time of year, so make sure to plan a few wildflower walks and camping expeditions.

Those in the Southeast United States have much to boast about this time of year: luscious sun-ripe raspberries, nectarines, and, of course, succulent juice-running-down-the-chin peaches. Make sure to preserve them all in this high-harvest season so you can enjoy them throughout the year.

At night in the Southwest, take part in the truly legendary stargazing that the big desert sky has to offer. Make sure to find a location away from any light pollution and allow your eyes at least twenty to thirty minutes to adjust.

The problem with summer is that it is oh-so fleeting, so enjoy it. Fall is just around the corner.

SUMMER

GROWING

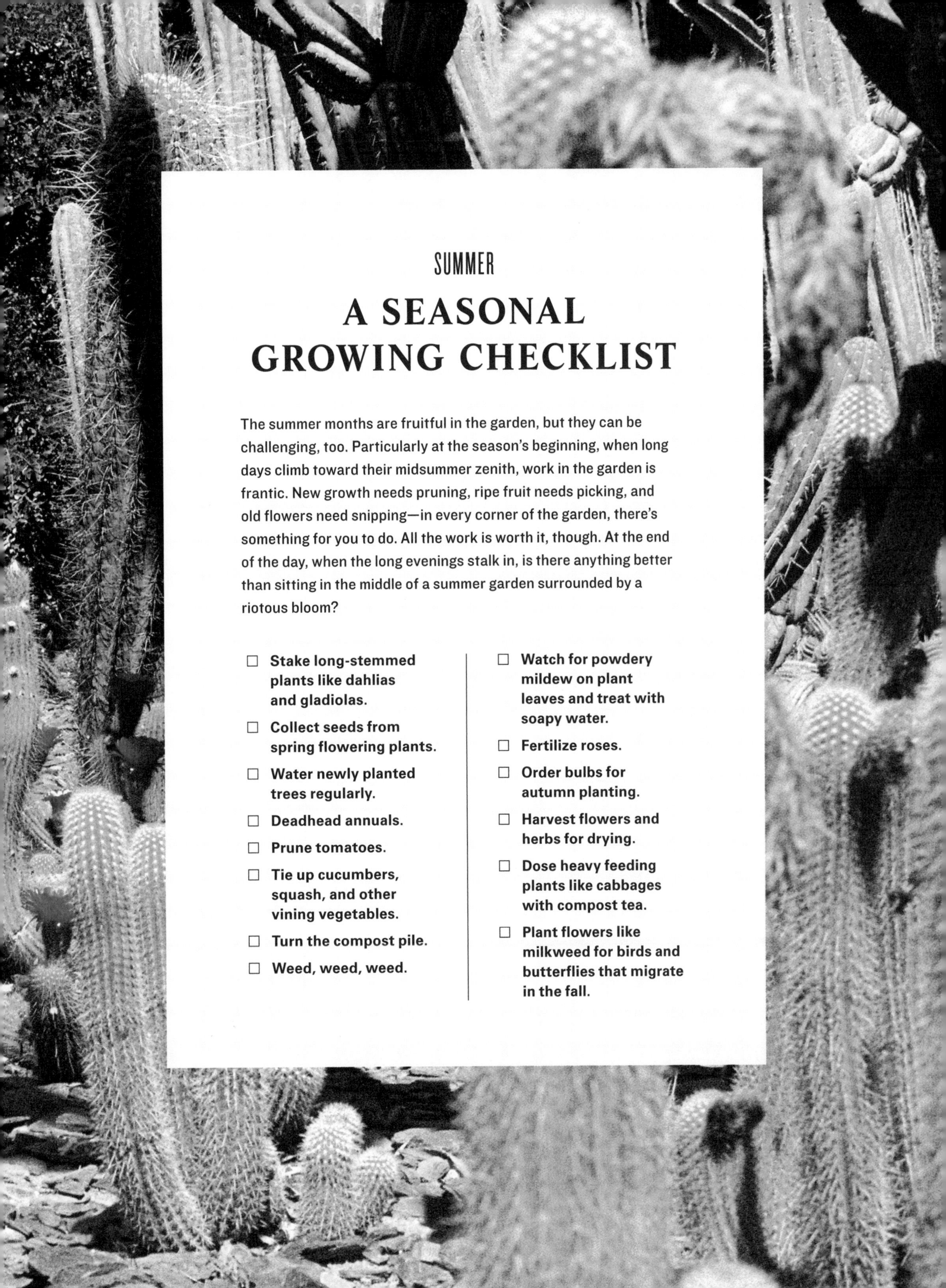

SUMMER

A SEASONAL GROWING CHECKLIST

The summer months are fruitful in the garden, but they can be challenging, too. Particularly at the season's beginning, when long days climb toward their midsummer zenith, work in the garden is frantic. New growth needs pruning, ripe fruit needs picking, and old flowers need snipping—in every corner of the garden, there's something for you to do. All the work is worth it, though. At the end of the day, when the long evenings stalk in, is there anything better than sitting in the middle of a summer garden surrounded by a riotous bloom?

- ☐ **Stake long-stemmed plants like dahlias and gladiolas.**
- ☐ **Collect seeds from spring flowering plants.**
- ☐ **Water newly planted trees regularly.**
- ☐ **Deadhead annuals.**
- ☐ **Prune tomatoes.**
- ☐ **Tie up cucumbers, squash, and other vining vegetables.**
- ☐ **Turn the compost pile.**
- ☐ **Weed, weed, weed.**
- ☐ **Watch for powdery mildew on plant leaves and treat with soapy water.**
- ☐ **Fertilize roses.**
- ☐ **Order bulbs for autumn planting.**
- ☐ **Harvest flowers and herbs for drying.**
- ☐ **Dose heavy feeding plants like cabbages with compost tea.**
- ☐ **Plant flowers like milkweed for birds and butterflies that migrate in the fall.**

COMMON NAME

Cup and saucer vine

LATIN NAME

Cobaea scandens

BLOOM TIME

Midsummer to fall

LIGHT

Full sun

SOIL

Semi-rich, freely draining soil

PESTS & PROBLEMS

Aphids, spider mites, seed-rot, if the weather is too cold and the soil too damp

BEST USE

As ground cover and for blooms

PLANT PROFILE

CUP AND SAUCER VINE

For some regions, summer is as fleeting as three short months, so when the season hits, put the pedal to the metal. Start cup and saucer vine (also known as cathedral bells, both for good reasons) in spring to have its purple bells ringing in your garden until fall. Its rapid growth and gorgeous outsized blooms will turn your garden into a tropical paradise.

Seeds

Cup and saucer seeds are as hard as porcelain. Although germination will occur within four weeks of planting, shoots appear in two weeks if seeds are soaked overnight. Plant seeds vertically, not flat, and barely cover with soil. Ideal soil temperature for the tropical *Cobaea scandens* ranges from 70° to 75°F, so if direct seeding outdoors, wait until the danger of frost has passed. If starting seeds indoors, begin six to eight weeks before the final frost date. Sow seeds in separate pots as young plants grow quickly.

Young Plants

Seedlings are extremely cold sensitive and are best kept indoors. If sowing outdoors, keep an eye on the weather: if temperatures dip below 50°F, provide protection, such as a covering of light fabric. Keep seedlings watered regularly, but don't allow the soil to remain wet. Do not fertilize young plants as this will promote rampant vine growth and fewer blossoms. Harden off new cup and saucer plants gradually, moving them outside on warm days (60°F and up) for an hour at a time, gradually increasing their exposure every day. Space plants two feet apart in a warm, sunny location protected from wind. Lightly mulch around the base of each plant to ensure good water retention.

Mature Plants

If treated right, cup and saucer vines will climb to twenty-five feet or more. No fertilizer is necessary to prompt this feat if situated in the right location; the vine is naturally an aggressive and rapid grower. In areas warm enough to grow the vine year round (zone 9, see Resources, page 265), cut back old stems every spring to coax more prolific flowering.

PLANT PROFILE

PAWPAW

With its long, glossy leaves and creamy oversized fruit, the tropical-looking pawpaw is a seductive addition to any fruit-lover's orchard. A relic of balmier, more humid times in North America, the pawpaw is cousin to South American sweetsop and cherimoya. The species is one of the only members of its family thriving outside the tropics and ranges all the way from riverbanks in Arkansas to the forests of Ontario. Scarlet spring-emergent flowers are beautiful, but conspicuously fetid to attract pollinating flies. The large fruits are theorized to have once been the diet of now extinct North American megafauna, a critter resembling the giant sloth. Adding a bit of historical significance to the plant, George Washington is rumored to have loved eating its fruit cold as a dessert.

Seeds

Cold stratified seeds germinate in midsummer. The long root will emerge within two to three weeks, with a shoot following a couple of months later. Success is best achieved by direct sowing outside: pawpaws do not transplant well.

Young Plants

Water young plants frequently during the first two years. Apply a balanced fertilizer during summer.

Mature Plants

Full-grown pawpaws require little maintenance but may need artificial pollination to ensure proper fruit set.

COMMON NAME

Pawpaw

LATIN NAME

Asimina triloba

FRUIT TIME

Late summer

LIGHT

Part sun

SOIL

Acidic, rich, freely draining soil

PESTS & PROBLEMS

Very few when planted in its native eastern range

BEST USE

Understory tree in woodland areas

KNOWLEDGE

IDENTIFYING GARDEN PESTS

Summer is the time for fruits and flowers. It's also, unfortunately, the time when garden pests multiply. Although general garden cleanliness, like weeding and pruning, goes a long way in preventing pests and pathogens, there are some troublemakers that require a little extra firepower to expunge them from the garden for good.

Crop rotation is a good place to start when managing pest problems. Vegetables, with their large attractive fruits and short growing season, are particularly susceptible to insect damage. Changing where vegetables are grown each year disrupts the life cycle of the pests that prey on them. For example, when young flea beetles emerge from the soil in spring and don't find food in the same place it was located last year, they die. For further protection from leaf eaters, floating row covers made of a light fabric and a hardy helping of mulch will go a long way toward limiting both their access to foliage and their emergence from the soil.

To stanch the damage done by fungi like black spot, powdery mildew, and early blight, keep beds squeaky clean. Most fungus is transported by wind, but cleaning up dead and diseased foliage and flowers prevents infecting spores from lingering nearby. Spacing plants evenly can increase air circulation, particularly in damp shaded areas, where this will help mitigate fungal growth, too.

For flying bugs, like aphids and whiteflies, spraying them with a dilute solution of soapy water coats their breathing holes and suffocates them. For larger, squashable critters like Japanese beetles or potato bugs, nothing does the trick like a pair of nimble fingers.

COMMON GARDEN PESTS, DISEASES, AND SUGGESTED REMEDIES

The following pests and pathogens are some of the most common and troublesome. Luckily, with a little persistence they are relatively easy to manage, too.

POWDERY MILDEW

WHAT IT IS: A white powdery fungus that thrives in dry weather

TARGET HOST: Nonspecific; affects everything from peonies and roses to cucumbers

TIME OF EMERGENCE: Mid- to late summer

REMEDY: Spray foliage with a dilute solution of soapy water

TOMATO HORNWORM

WHAT IT IS: The larvae of a large, native hawk moth

TARGET HOST: Vegetables in the tomato family and native plants in the Jimson weed genus

TIME OF EMERGENCE: Mid- to late summer

REMEDY: Rotate tomatoes each year; pull larvae from plants, then squash or relocate the larvae

FLEA BEETLE

WHAT IT IS: A tiny, jumping black to gray beetle

TARGET HOST: Nonspecific; everything from eggplant to cabbage

TIME OF EMERGENCE: Early to midsummer

REMEDY: Lay fresh mulch in spring; cover susceptible plants with a floating row

JAPANESE BEETLE

WHAT IT IS: A glossy, iridescent, half-inch-long beetle

TARGET HOST: Mainly roses, but will feed on most flowers and foliage

TIME OF EMERGENCE: Early summer

REMEDY: Collect adults early in the morning and drop into soapy water; spread nematodes, a kind of parasitic worm, to target larvae in fall

APHID

WHAT IT IS: A small green insect with sucking mouthparts

TARGET HOST: Nonspecific; targets new, tender plant growth such as flower buds

TIME OF EMERGENCE: Late spring to early summer

REMEDY: Spray insects with a dilute solution of soapy water

SQUASH BORER

WHAT IT IS: The larvae of a native clearwing moth

TARGET HOST: Members of the squash family

TIME OF EMERGENCE: Mid- to late summer

REMEDY: Cover plants with a floating row to prevent adults from laying eggs on them; carefully pull existing larvae out from stem tissue

BLACK SPOT

WHAT IT IS: A fungus that creates unsightly black spots on foliage

TARGET HOST: Roses

TIME OF EMERGENCE: Late summer, or whenever cooler, moist weather arrives

REMEDY: Plant roses in sunny areas with good air circulation, and use organic fungicidal sprays preventively

SKILL

HOW TO CREATE A NIGHT-BLOOMING GARDEN

When night falls, not everything goes to sleep. In fact, a number of plants use the dark, cool cover of night to tend to vital functions, like transpiration and reproduction. The Saguaro cactus opens its creamy petals to let in nectar-drinking bats, while night-blooming water lilies unfold for moths. A whole world of wildlife and flowers thrives beneath the inky cover of darkness. Here's how to create—and really enjoy—a night-blooming garden.

1. PLAN FOR VARIETY. Select an array of plants that will attract different types of animals and bugs: some night bloomers attract bats, while others are irresistible to moths. Don't forget to plant flowers that will lure humans from the house as their scents drift in through a bedroom window.

2. PLANT CLOSE TO THE HOUSE. Generally speaking, gardeners are early-bird types. Situate the night garden somewhere close by—near the fire pit, grill, or, even better, right next to the front porch—so it's easy to enjoy.

3. USE SMALLER PLANTS. Create border beds along the house or patio and plant low or mounding annuals and perennials, like brightly colored four o'clocks or the larger devil's trumpets, there. Remember, smaller plants make a big impact when planted en masse.

4. UTILIZE VINES IN INTERESTING WAYS. Several night-blooming vines, such as moonflower, are an almost inconspicuous tangle of green during the day. Train them along larger day blooming shrubs to lend extra height and layers to the night garden.

5. HANG AND LAY OUT POTS. Striking specimens such as night-blooming cereus and even yucca deserve to be shown off. Placing pots near seating areas, such as on the porch, make it easier to observe large and showy moths when they zoom in for a drink.

6. GIVE EACH FLOWER SPACE. Many night bloomers have strong fragrances to compensate for the low visibility of their flowers in the darkness. Space plants out a bit so no one fragrance is competing with, or overpowering, another.

OUR FAVORITE NIGHT BLOOMERS

Sporting luminous blooms and full-bodied scents, these selections are also extremely attractive to wildlife and will bring the night to life.

MOONFLOWER (*Ipomoea alba*)

BEST USE: Twining on a trellis or day-blooming bush; attracts moths.

NIGHT-BLOOMING JASMINE (*Cestrum nocturnum*)

BEST USE: Grown on a fence or in a large pot and placed close to a window; attracts moths and beetles.

NIGHT-BLOOMING CEREUS (*Nyctocereus serpentinus*)

BEST USE: Hanging in pots near doorways; attracts moths and bats.

EVENING PRIMROSE (*Oenothera biennis*)

BEST USE: Grown in large swaths and naturalized in meadows; attracts moths.

FOUR O'CLOCK (*Mirabalis jalapa*)

BEST USE: Grown in borders; attracts moths.

WATER LILY (*Nymphaea*)

BEST USE: Grown densely in shallow ponds or ornamental buckets on porches; attracts beetles and moths.

TOBACCO (*Nicotiana*)

BEST USE: Grown in pots or in borders; attracts moths.

YUCCA (*Yucca*)

BEST USE: Naturalized in a meadow; attracts moths.

SKILL

HOW TO HAND POLLINATE

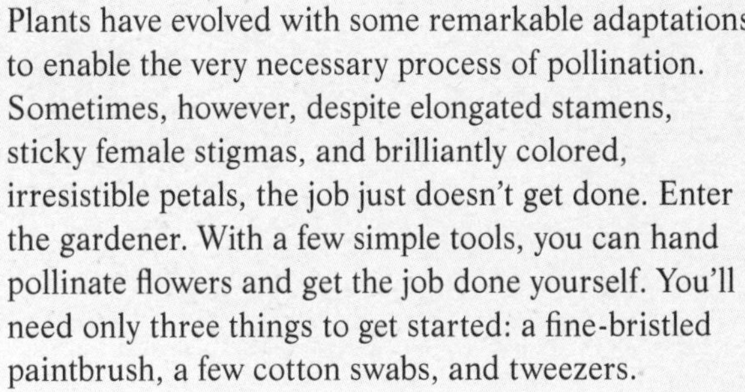

Plants have evolved with some remarkable adaptations to enable the very necessary process of pollination. Sometimes, however, despite elongated stamens, sticky female stigmas, and brilliantly colored, irresistible petals, the job just doesn't get done. Enter the gardener. With a few simple tools, you can hand pollinate flowers and get the job done yourself. You'll need only three things to get started: a fine-bristled paintbrush, a few cotton swabs, and tweezers.

1. MAKE A PLAN. Identify plants that may need a helping hand early in the season to make sure you don't miss their flowering period. Flowers that are dioecious (i.e., that do not produce a single plant with both male and female parts) often need to be hand pollinated to set fruit, unless there is a partner of the opposite sex nearby. Hollies, persimmons, and some currants fall into this category. Remember, for the overwhelming majority of plants, only individuals of the same species can interbreed.

2. GET AN EARLY START. Collect pollen in the morning when flowers first open, and before insects like bees are out performing their own pollination rituals. The pollen will be freshest at this time of day, too.

3. GATHER THE RIGHT TOOLS. A cotton swab or a very fine-bristled paintbrush will hold pollen well. Collect pollen by rubbing the brush or swab very gently over the stamens, which should be bright yellow-orange.

4. ACT QUICKLY. Transfer the collected pollen to the stigma, the pollen receptacle on the flower's female organ, as soon as possible; pollen dries out quickly if left in the open air for too long. Generally, the stigma is located in the middle of the flower, and often projects beyond the pollen-caked stamens. Many receptive flowers will have an obviously sticky, glossy stigma when ready. Brush the yellow pollen grains gently onto the stigma. They should easily attach. Repeat the process for all open flowers. After the flower senesces and dies, you literally should be able to see the fruits of your labor swelling and developing where the flower once bloomed.

SUMMER

COOKING

SUMMER

INGREDIENTS TO INSPIRE

Fruits

APRICOTS
BLACKBERRIES
BLUEBERRIES
BOYSENBERRIES
CHERRIES
CURRANTS (WHITE AND RED)
FIGS
MELONS (CANTALOUPE, WATERMELON, HONEYDEW)
MULBERRIES
NECTARINES (WHITE AND RED)
PEACHES (WHITE AND YELLOW)
PEARS
PLUMS
PLUOTS
RASPBERRIES
TAYBERRIES

Vegetables

BEETS
BELL PEPPERS (GREEN, RED, YELLOW, ORANGE, WHITE, PURPLE)
BROCCOLI
CARROTS
CHILI PEPPERS
CHINESE LONG BEANS
CORN
CUCUMBERS (PICKLING, ENGLISH)
DRAGON TONGUE BEANS
EGGPLANT
FENNEL
GARLIC
GREEN SOYBEANS
HERBS (THYME, SAGE, PARSLEY, CILANTRO, ROSEMARY, CHIVES, DILL, MINT, BASIL)
HUNGARIAN HOT PEPPERS
JALAPEÑOS
KALE
LEEKS
LETTUCES
LIMA BEANS
MUSHROOMS (PORTOBELLO, CREMINI, SHIITAKE, MAITAKE, CHANTERELLE)
OKRA
ONIONS (WALLA WALLA, RED, WHITE)
PEAS
POTATOES
RADISHES
SHALLOTS
SPINACH
SQUASH
STRING BEANS
SWEET PEPPERS
TOMATILLOS
TOMATOES (ALL VARIETIES)
ZUCCHINI

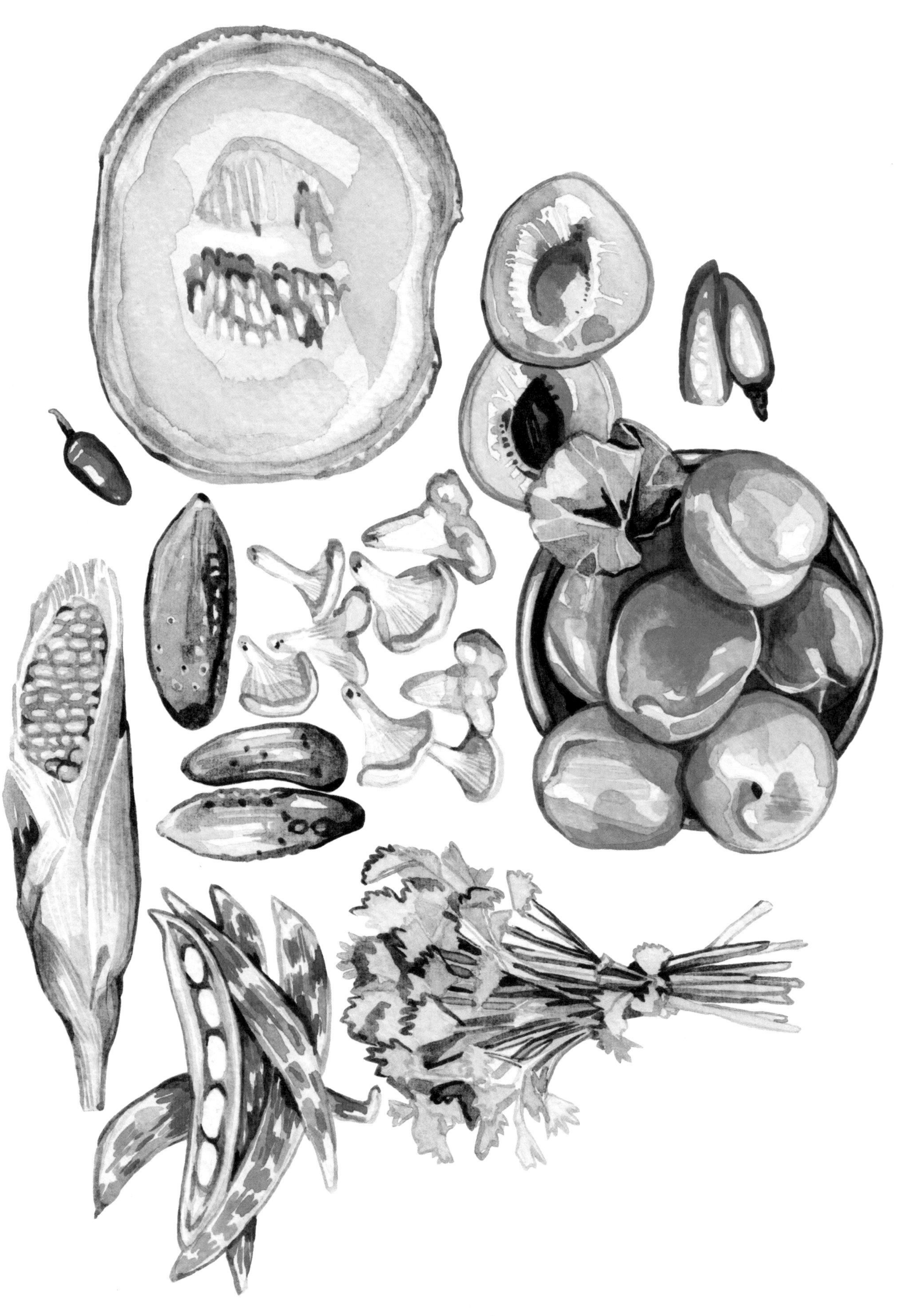

KNOWLEDGE

A PRIMER ON CANNING

Fruit doesn't stay as perfect as we know it from first squeeze for very long—nor do mid-February tomatoes taste the same as August's luscious harvest. While there is no magic way to bottle the feeling of biting into a softly yielding raspberry warmed by the sun, there are well-traversed ways to preserve the flavors of the season long past the sunset of summer.

Why Can?

Aside from the aforementioned taste factor, preserving seasonal harvests allows you to eat within your region all year long. This means limiting your reliance on imported, or at least well-traveled, produce, and by proxy reducing your carbon footprint and potential reliance on the larger agribusiness system. Frequently, this also means that your produce costs will be cheaper in the long run—buying in season when produce is abundant and local versus paying for a tomato in January in Rhode Island that has been shipped to you from California. Plus, incorporating short-season treats like ramps, scapes, and fiddleheads allows you to keep a little of the magic of that season throughout the year.

How Does It Work?

Produce spoils because unwanted microorganisms take up residence in your perfectly ripe fruits or vegetables, and begin to break them down. These organisms need conditions not unlike our own to be able to thrive: oxygen, water, temperatures between 40° and 139°F, and an environment that is low in acid. If you eliminate one or a few of these conditions, fresh produce will last longer.

Preserving Methods

There are a few ways to extend the season. Drying herbs, fruits, and produce will take the water out of the equation. Freezing will slow down the growth of microorganisms (but not eliminate them completely). Acidulating (or pickling) fresh produce via vinegar, lemon juice, or fermentation will create an environment too acidic for unwanted new growth—although in most cases it will still need to be processed.

Canning is brilliant because it eliminates most of the factors necessary for microorganisms to thrive: You apply heat when you process your jars in either a hot water bath or a pressure cooker. You eliminate oxygen by creating a vacuum seal on the jar. And you create an environment that has enough acid to keep unwelcome growth at bay. That triple threat makes it possible to leave jars in a cupboard at comfortable household temperatures without having the food spoil.

How to Can Using a Hot Water Bath

Canning seems mysterious at first, but in fact is quite simple. Using the hot-water-bath method, you will be able to can jams, jellies, preserves, sauces, pickles, chutneys, and fruit butters. To can low-acid foods like unacidulated vegetables and meats, you will need to use a pressure cooker or else run the risk of botulism or the invasion of those pesky microorganisms.

Begin by placing your Mason jars in a water bath and completely covering them with water. When the water is at a rolling boil, cook for ten minutes—this will sterilize the jars. When they have properly "cooked," place the jars upside down on the counter on a clean, dry tea towel. Keep your water bath boiling.

Meanwhile, prepare whatever is going to go into the jars (see our recipes for sauerkraut on page 226, preserves on pages 103 and 106, and fruit butter on page 167). Once your mixture is ready, use a funnel to fill the jars, leaving a quarter inch or less of headspace at the top of each jar—you want to leave as little room for oxygen as possible. Take a damp paper towel and wipe the rim of your jar clean. Place the lid on top and, using your jar lifter, place the jars (right side up) back in your water bath, taking care to make sure they are covered by at least one inch of boiling water. Boil your jars for ten minutes and then turn off the heat to your water bath and allow the jars to sit in the water for an additional ten minutes. Remove the jars using your jar lifter and let them rest on a countertop uninterrupted for at least twelve hours.

That's it! Sterilize your jars, fill them with something delicious, clean the tops, boil them again, and enjoy summer (or spring or fall) all year long.

WHAT YOU'LL NEED FOR CANNING

HOT WATER BATH: Use a simple stock pot; make sure the bath is large enough to accommodate all of the jars you want to process and deep enough that they can be covered by at least one inch of water.

JAR LIFTER: This piece of equipment is nonnegotiable. Tongs will work in a pinch, but jars can be slippery. Save yourself the hassle of dealing with potential hot glass breakage and purchase a jar lifter

MASON JARS: The lids of Mason jars will compress to let you know that the vacuum-seal has been set, and the mouths of the jars are usually measured to fit most funnels.

WIDEMOUTHED FUNNEL: A funnel is essential for ensuring that your mixture makes it into the jar and not onto the sides of the jar, where it could fall outside of your vacuum seal and attract microorganisms.

RECIPE

MAKE RABBIT'S GINGER PEAR SAUCE

We could wax poetic for an eternity about the virtues of jams, jellies, and preserves. They are a world unto themselves and deserving of many more pages than this. But when we think long and hard about it, there really is only one preserve we'd take with us to a desert island: Rabbit's Ginger Pear Sauce. We love and cherish many others—and make plenty of their compatriots all summer long—but this is the one we couldn't bear to live without.

In Abbye's mom's kitchen, ginger pear sauce was present all year round, crowning fruit salads and chocolate desserts and lending sweet spiciness to roast pork.

For Celestine, the discovery of this sauce came later in life—around pregnancy, to be exact. Something about the tart sweetness made it less like a condiment and more like a calling around the third trimester.

Below is Abbye's mom's Rabbit's Ginger Pear Sauce recipe.

INGREDIENTS

8 cups peeled, chopped Bartlett pears (about 14 medium pears)

4½ cups sugar

2 tablespoons powdered ginger

1 lemon, peeled, seeded, white membranes removed and chopped

One 8½-ounce can crushed pineapple, drained

EQUIPMENT

Large mixing bowl

Water bath

Six 8-ounce Mason jars

3 small plates

6- to 8-quart preserving pan or shallow pan

Ladle

Widemouthed funnel

Paper towels

Jar lifter or tongs

Tea towels

Blender or food processor (optional)

Makes 6 pints

DIRECTIONS

1. Combine the chopped pears, sugar, and powdered ginger in a bowl, toss, and let stand for at least 2 hours.

2. Prepare a hot water bath and sterilize your jars (for instructions, see page 101).

3. Place the pear mixture in a pan and slowly bring to a boil over medium heat. Reduce the heat to low and continue cooking for about 15 minutes.

4. Mix in the chopped lemon and crushed pineapple. Continue to cook for another 30 minutes, stirring occasionally so as not to burn the bottom. It's done cooking when the liquid has reduced and the texture is like that of thick applesauce. This recipe will not set up like a jam, but rather will retain the texture of a thick sauce. Ladle the jam into the sterilized jars using a funnel.

5. Wipe the rims with a damp paper towel, add the lids, and process the jars in boiling water for 15 minutes.

6. Remove the jars using a jar lifter and allow them to rest on a tea towel untouched overnight. Once processed, kept in a dark cupboard, the sauce will be shelf-stable for up to one year. Refrigerate after opening and use within 1 month.

RECIPE

MAKE AN ALL-PURPOSE TOMATO SAUCE

There's nothing as distinctly summery—or as fleeting—as a vine-ripe tomato. The juicy, tangy fruit is at its apex in the high summer heat and compared to the ones lining supermarket shelves in midwinter, might as well be a different fruit. February's mealy, flavorless pink mush doesn't hold a candle to August's bittersweet, slightly acidic, juice-running-down-your-chin tomato. Make use of this ample seasonal supply and stow away as much of the good stuff as you can.

Canned fruits and vegetables are only ever as good as the produce you start with, so make sure you find superlative fruit. Tomatoes ripen from the bottom up, so look for the glossy red to extend through to the shoulders to tell if the tomato is ripe. Never refrigerate tomatoes after harvesting as it will change the flavor. Opt instead for countertop storage in a brown paper bag, if necessary; or better yet, bring them straight from the vine to the pot.

For this recipe, we subscribe to Italian goddess chef Lidia Bastianich's philosophy: "It takes work to get to simplicity." This simple basic sauce uses scant ingredients, but doctored with a few additional ones, it can become a base for marinara sauce, enchilada sauce, tomato soup, beef stew, braising sauce, pizza sauce, sofrito, curry, ketchup . . . you get the idea. This recipe will fill one 24-ounce jar (roughly a pasta sauce jar's worth), but we recommend doubling it (or more!) to stock your pantry for the year to come.

INGREDIENTS

3 pounds plum tomatoes
3 tablespoons olive oil
½ medium onion, chopped
4 large garlic cloves, slivered
½ tablespoon kosher salt, or to taste
½ tablespoon ground pepper
½ tablespoon chili flakes

EQUIPMENT

Large pot
Large bowl
Slotted spoon
Skillet
Blender or food processor
Hot water bath
Tea towel
Ladle
24-ounce jar
Widemouthed funnel
Paper towels
Jar lifter

DIRECTIONS

1. Fill a large pot with water and bring to a boil. Fill a large bowl with ice water and set aside.

2. When the water boils, one by one, using a slotted spoon, submerge each tomato for about 30 seconds and then place immediately in the ice bath. This will help loosen the skins of the tomatoes so they can be easily peeled without fully cooking them.

3. Peel the tomatoes and, using your hands, pull apart their flesh to remove the seeds and core. Reserve the flesh in a separate bowl. Discard the peels and seeds.

4. Add the olive oil to a skillet on medium heat. Add the onion and let it cook until it is translucent and tender, about 10 minutes.

5. Add the tomato flesh and cook for 5 minutes.

6. Remove the mixture from the heat and add it to a food processor or blender; blend until velvety and smooth.

7. Return the mixture to the skillet, add the slivered garlic, and cook over medium heat. Season with salt, pepper, and chili. Simmer until the sauce changes to a deep ruby red color, stirring frequently, about 40 minutes.

8. While the sauce is cooking, prepare the hot water bath and sterilize your jar (or jars).

9. Set the jar upside down on a tea towel.

10. Ladle the sauce into the sterilized jar using a funnel.

11. Wipe the rim with a damp paper towel, add the lid, and process the jar in boiling water for 15 minutes.

12. Remove the jar using a jar lifter and allow to rest on a towel untouched overnight. Once processed, kept in a dark cupboard, the sauce will be shelf-stable for up to one year. Refrigerate after opening and use within 2 weeks.

HOME & SELF-RELIANCE

SUMMER

PREPARE YOUR HOME FOR THE SEASON

In summer, we're in full swing, basking in the sun, relishing the season, and hoping that all our hard work from the three seasons prior was enough to prepare for nature's busiest time. There's still plenty to do in this high season, but make sure to leave time for the summer's most important task: enjoying it!

- ☐ **Make use of this prolific time by adding kitchen scraps and garden trimmings regularly to your compost pile (see page 117).**
- ☐ **Switch to summer bedding and use drawn shades or curtains to limit the sun's heat and reduce the need for air-conditioning.**
- ☐ **Bring the garden indoors with flower arrangements (see page 114).**
- ☐ **Put up summer fruit and vegetables (see page 100).**
- ☐ **Chop and freeze herbs in ice cube trays for year-round use in cooking.**
- ☐ **Take advantage of the extended hours of sunlight to cut down on the use of indoor electric lights.**
- ☐ **Move potted indoor plants outdoors to take advantage of the new angle and intensity of the summer sun.**
- ☐ **Repot any houseplants that have outgrown their containers.**
- ☐ **Chop wood for the woodpile.**
- ☐ **Ensure proper air circulation in barns and coops—hot weather allows bacteria to breed in confined spaces.**
- ☐ **Test eggs for calcium deficiency by gently squeezing their shells—if they crack, feed your chickens a calcium-rich shell mix for the summer.**
- ☐ **Place poultry in any new garden areas before planting to till the soil and eat any weeds.**
- ☐ **Prune back poisonous plants emerging in a pasture, like black swallow wort and leafy spurge.**
- ☐ **Mix a natural insect repellent using foraged plants like spicebush or wild mint.**
- ☐ **Plan an evening event in your night-blooming garden (see page 92).**

AN INTRODUCTION TO IKEBANA

Summer's overabundant blooms can fill you with dumbstruck awe as bursts of color splash against a verdant carpet of foliage—filigreed delicate petals, thick and waxy green leaves, tall spires of grasses. Make the most of this diverse season by bringing nature's beauty indoors through the Japanese practice of ikebana.

Ikebana is commonly translated as "to preserve living flowers" and is part of the broader study of *kado,* the way of the flowers. Many believe this traditional art form of Japan began as a Buddhist spiritual practice where flowers were arranged before being offered to spirits that had passed on or to honor Buddha. Other schools of thought believe that the practice of ikebana predates Buddhism in Japan. Whatever its origins, by the fifteenth century, ikebana had transcended its devotional origins to become an art form in its own right, though many of the principles of Buddhism—peace, harmony, respect, and a reverence for daily life—are integral to the understanding of ikebana today.

There are many different schools of ikebana, but the guiding principles of the practice have remained the same for centuries. In ikebana, it is believed that flowers have their own inherent sculptural form. Just as Michelangelo believed that every block of stone has a statue inside it and it is the task of the sculptor to discover it, in ikebana the practitioner works with natural elements to unveil their voice and form. For this reason, silence is required when practicing ikebana so that the practitioner can observe nature and tune in to the inherent form. In this meditative practice, the essential aspects of individual stems, branches, and flowers are revealed, with particular attention paid to the truest expression of line and shape in each element.

The elements are then assembled into a triangular structure with three main parts: *shin* (the tallest point of your arrangement, representing heaven), *soc* (the medium-sized point of your arrangement, representing man), and *hikae* (the lowest point of your arrangement, representing earth). The stems of these three elements are placed in a *kenzan,* or pinholder tool, which supports the plant material and helps it to stand upright. Different styles of ikebana will dictate the placement of the elements within the kenzan. Traditionally, the kenzan is not attached to the container or vase and it is never placed in the middle.

Once the three main parts are placed in the kenzan, any number of *jushi*—or additional flowers, leaves, and stems—can be placed within the arrangement as long as they are kept to an odd number; it is believed an even number will bring conflict without resolution. Color, structure, line, and form, as well as the expressiveness of the plants, are all considered as a practitioner creates an arrangement.

Arranging flowers can become an emotional and psychologically rewarding process, as you see yourself and your struggles reflected in the flowers. Ikebana strives to create a moment of stillness that can engender a dialogue between beauty, aesthetics, emotion, and human understanding.

THE BASIC RULES OF IKEBANA

Ikebana is a lifelong meditative practice, and as with any good practice, thorough reading and research is necessary to fully understand its intricacies and get the most from your practice. As a foundation to this understanding, and to reveal deeper meaning, here are a few rules of ikebana, though we encourage you to seek out a teacher or a good book to broaden your understanding. See Resources on page 265 for further reading.

- Always know the names of your flowers; it is a sign of disrespect not to.
- Always work in an odd number of elements; odd numbers offer a solution, whereas even numbers add confusion.
- Always work with the plant's natural shape and form; be true to what exists naturally.
- Incorporate a diversity of stem widths; different widths promote diversity and create an opportunity for harmony.
- Prune back leaves or flowers directly across from one another to avoid conflict.
- Arrange flowers so that every part is visible, never overlapping; the strengths of each element should stand out.

A PRIMER ON COMPOSTING

Compost is nothing short of alchemy: mix shredded cardboard, some old leaves, and an armful of twigs with the scraps from the garden and the kitchen. The result? Black gold. Really, compost is the panacea of all garden ailments. Waterlogged soil? Add compost. Too dry? Add compost! Flagging and unhealthy plants? More compost! The heady, heavy, dark stuff can even be brewed into a tea and sprayed on foliage to prevent damage from pests like aphids (plant lice). Clearly, with so many benefits, it pays to get down in the dirt and learn how to make your own.

The rule of thumb to follow for every compost recipe is three parts brown to two parts green. "Brown" materials like fallen leaves and wood chips are rich in carbon and ensure that compost is well aerated. "Green" materials such as veggie scraps and garden trimmings provide nitrogen—a vital nutrient for all plants. Keep this ratio in mind as the pile starts to grow come midsummer.

Choose a shaded spot close to the garden to get started. If animals like raccoons are a problem, consider erecting a pallet barrier or some other protection to keep the pile properly partitioned. As material is added, ensure that the compost mixture stays moist by mixing from the bottom of the pile to maintain maximum decomposition rates. To create a thriving compost, and to kill weed seeds, add animal manure. Goat, chicken, rabbit, and horse manure works particularly well but must be completely broken down before it's put on a vegetable garden. This can take six months to a year. Remember to never compost dog droppings. In fact, keep carnivore droppings out of the equation entirely. Any oily foods or dairy products should be left out, too—not just because they can leave hard-to-break-down fatty residues in compost, but because they'll also attract unwanted wildlife to the pile.

Turning the pile with a garden fork once a week will accelerate decomposition and encourage good mixing. Generally speaking, the process from garden refuse to riches takes several months at least. To be sure the pile has made its final transformation, check for uniform composition throughout the pile. None of the original ingredients should be recognizable—and they certainly shouldn't smell. Good compost is dark, moist, crumbly, and virtually odorless. Before planting in new compost, spread it over the surface of the planting site and wait a week. This will let the mixture steadily work its way into the soil and perform the earthy magic that only compost can do.

COMPOSTING DO'S AND DON'TS

Think twice before you toss it in the bin. Here's a list of what to compost and what to chuck.

MATERIALS TO COMPOST	MATERIALS TO AVOID
Algae, seaweed	Citrus fruit
Banana peels	Coal ashes
Beverages	Colored paper
Cardboard	Dairy products
Coffee filters	Diseased plants
Coffee grounds	Dog or cat excrement
Corncobs	Grease
Dog food	Meat and animal parts
Dryer lint	Nonbiodegradable materials
Eggshells	
Fruit (not citrus)	
Grass clippings	
Hay	
Leaves	
Paper	
Plant matter	
Tea	
Unused cat litter	
Vegetable scraps	
Weeds	
Wood ashes	

DIY

MAKE YOUR OWN SUMMER SANDALS

Making shoes falls into the same category as pigs flying or a certain nether-region freezing over: file under impossible. We have come a long way from thinking about human hands measuring, sculpting, carving, and stitching our footwear. With the insane diversity of shoes available on the market—from teetering, perilous stilettos to combat boots beaten-up with precision—it is hard to imagine shoes being made by hand. And with the unique tools required, the art of making shoes has always seemed out of reach for the layperson.

Thankfully, there are contemporary artisans like Los Angeles–based Beatrice Valenzuela who are bringing back this art form. When starting to make your own shoes, Beatrice advises to "think about what your favorite shoe is, find really soft leather, and go from there." The pattern below, created by Beatrice, is based on a slip-on sandal. You can make this simple design with just a few tools and an eye for precision.

WHAT YOU'LL NEED

Marker

Construction paper

One 1-square-foot piece of leather

One 1-square-foot piece of rubber (choose any thickness and source you like)

Leather scissors

Leather hole puncher

Leather needle

Cotton string

Leather cement glue

Clamps or a heavy book

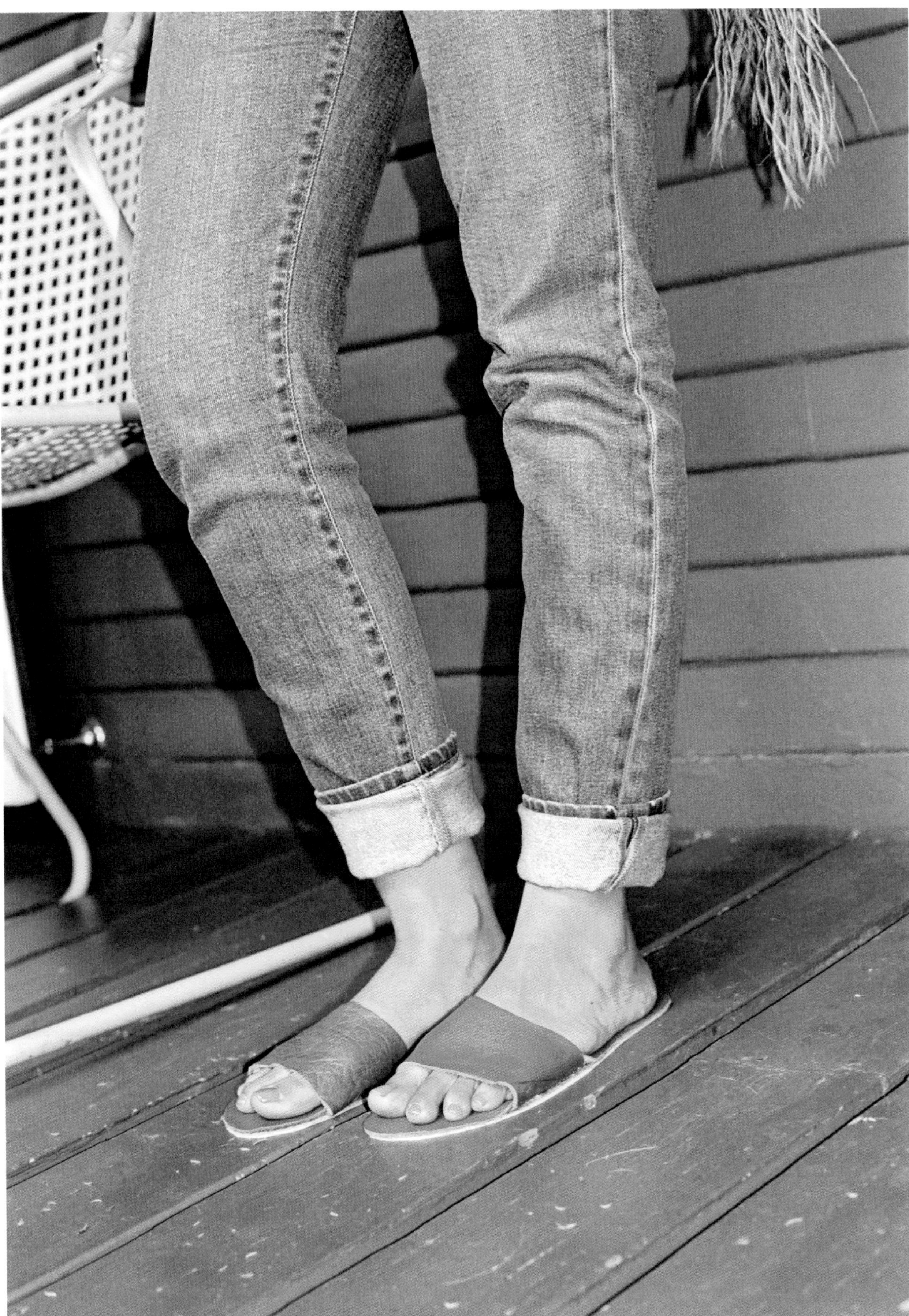

DIRECTIONS

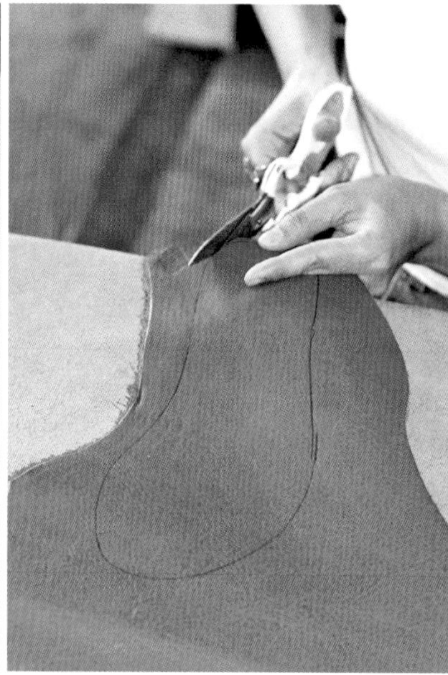

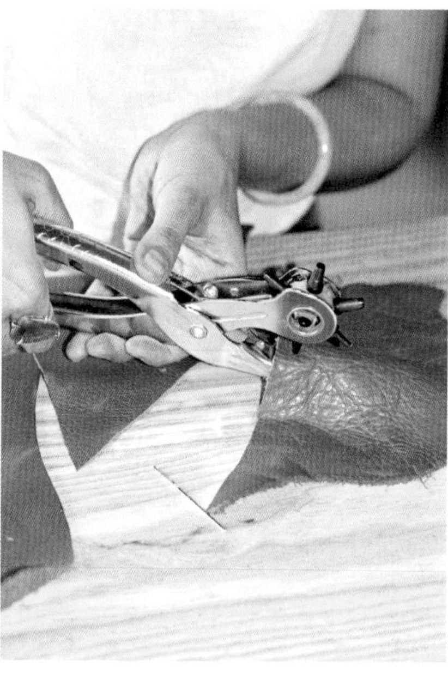

1. Using a marker, trace the shape of both your feet (or those of the person you're making the sandals for) on a piece of construction paper.

2. Trace the template onto the leather and the rubber for both feet. Cut out all the pieces with scissors. Cut two leather strips, each 2 to 3 inches wide, from the remaining scrap of leather. These straps will become the top part of the sandal.

3. Punch several holes in the two strips and the foot-bed leather. These holes should line up where you want your straps to attach to the sole and be large enough to accommodate a leather string (see next step).

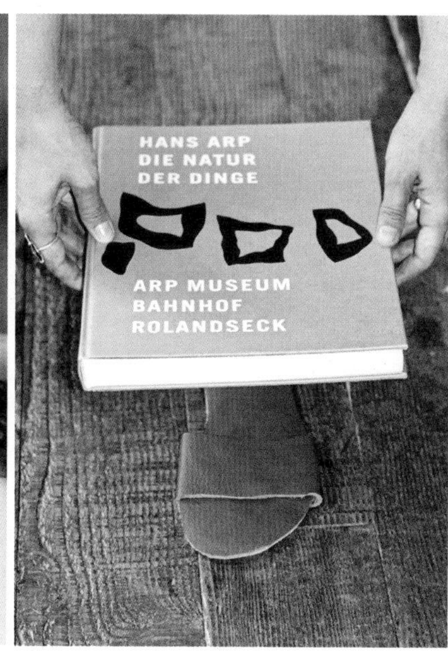

4. From your remaining leather, cut long, skinny pieces that will form your leather string (about the width of shoelaces).

5. Use a leather needle and the leather strings to sew the foot-bed piece to the top straps. Sew using a whipstitch on one side of the sandal and mirror that on the other side. Then repeat that stitch with the cotton string, making a whipstitch in the opposite direction from the leather string so that the leather string and cotton string alternate (leather in/cotton out of a hole and vice versa until you reach the end of the strap). Repeat with the other sandal.

6. Use the cement glue to adhere the foot-bed leather to the rubber soles.

7. Secure the pieces together using clamps or weight them with heavy books. Follow the manufacturer's directions for the glue dry time.

SUMMER

BEAUTY & HEALING

KNOWLEDGE

A SEASONAL APOTHECARY

Temperatures and humidity run high in the summer. Skin can become aggravated by overexposure to sun, heat, and the bites of pesky insects. Blood circulates quickly, leading to irritation and classic "hot tempers." Thankfully this sun-drenched season also provides enough blossoms and blooms to counteract the season's ailments. Capitalize on the bounty of the season with refreshing flowers and herbs that detoxify the body, inside and out. Here are a few of our favorites.

HERBS TO TONE AND DETOXIFY

Tea Tree Oil
Antiviral and antifungal; excellent for use with rashes, skin infections, and insect bites. Use as a salve or medicinal oil.

Witch Hazel
Astringent and drying to the skin; helpful for blemishes and blisters. Use as an infusion.

HERBS TO COOL AND CALM	HERBS TO SOOTHE SKIN
 **Peppermint and Spearmint** Has a cooling effect internally and externally. Use as a tea, culinary herb, or salve.	 **Aloe Vera** Cools and tones the skin externally; eases pain from sunburns or heat rash. Apply the gel directly to affected areas.
 **Rose** Astringent and anti-inflammatory; cools the skin and the body. Use as an infusion topically.	 **Burdock** Calming and cooling to irritated skin; especially useful in treating eczema and rashes. Drink as a tea or apply a cloth soaked in the tea directly to the skin.
 **Violet** Helps calm the nervous system thanks to naturally occurring salicylic acid (i.e., aspirin); externally, helps relieve irritated skin and rosacea. Use as a culinary herb or as an infused oil.	 **Chickweed** Relieves itchy skin, rashes, and dry skin. Use as a salve.

KNOWLEDGE

A PRIMER ON HEALING STONES

Think of crystals and stereotypical images come to mind: the silver-ring-adorned elder hippie, the iconic Alex Gray chakra chart, or perhaps a certain Pink Floyd album cover. While these symbols are most definitely part of the culture of crystal healing, they are only the most recent additions to the long-held beliefs in the powers of stones. The ancient Egyptians thought that wearing amulets of precious stones would protect them from evil spirits and also from poisoned wine; ancient Chinese civilizations have attributed cultural meaning to jade since the Neolithic period; Native American cultures have used stones and crystals as spiritual tools in ceremonies for centuries; and medieval shields and armor incorporated gemstones as a sign of wealth and adornment.

Today, we have scientific evidence that crystals transmit energy—quartz-movement watches utilize crystal oscillators to regulate precise time, electronics-grade crystals can be used in cell phones, TVs, and computers. In the belief system of crystal healing, the same principles of focusing and transmitting energy are applied to the body or spirit.

Different cultures use crystals and gemstones differently—some complementary therapies encourage placing the stones on the body to connect to the body's energy fields or chakras, while others prefer the use of wands or pendulums. As nature lovers, we prefer to appreciate the stones for what they are: marvels of nature.

Here is a selection of our favorite stones along with some of the healing beliefs associated with them. To make use of their beauty (or to harness their energies, if you like), we recommend wearing them, placing them in your home, or using the crystals as meditation objects. Whatever your beliefs might be, the beauty of crystals' magical formation is without question.

Amethyst
Calming; facilitates meditation, spiritual awareness, and inner peace; deepens intuition

Hematite
Stone of protection; grounds emotions and anxiety

Garnet
Helps to strengthen and enhance physicality and sexual drive; stimulates internal fire

Jade
Traditional good luck stone; inspires ambition; brings wealth

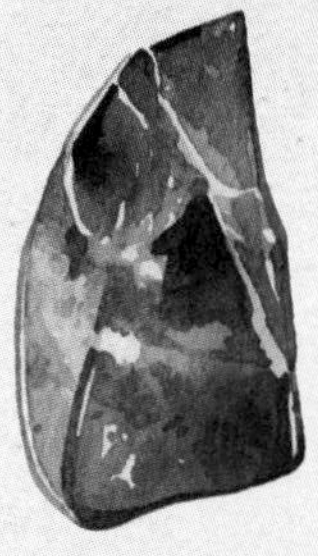

Lapis Lazuli
Used in the courts of Egyptian kings; intensifies the intellect and deepens wisdom; promotes clear communication

Rose Quartz
The stone of unconditional love, both platonic and romantic; gives a sense of peace in relationships; nurturing, peaceful energy; enhances one's ability to give and receive love

Moonstone
Opens up creativity, perception, and sensitivity; good for increasing one's intuitive abilities and humanitarian love

Smoky Quartz
Brings light to the body and spirit; helps ground negative thoughts; helpful for those who are afraid to take risks or prone to overindulgence

Obsidian
Stone of transformation; assists in making deep inner changes and facing fears

Tiger's Eye
Relieves uncertainty; encourages integrity; helps provide ability to see clearly

Pink Kunzite
The stone of healing; helps penetrate emotional blockages and open the heart; helps release creativity

DIY

HOW TO BLEND YOUR OWN PERFUME

There are many reasons to make your own perfume—quality control of its ingredients and saving money among them—but the most compelling reason is that the perfume you make will be your scent alone, imitated by no one. Create your own perfume and you'll have a scent that is distinctly you.

Fair warning: achieving the exact smell you seek requires a good deal of trial and error, so have patience. Getting to know your ingredients first is key to developing the ability to blend your ideal scent. Any perfume is created by a combination of notes—top, middle, and base—which work together to create an accord or harmony. The top note is usually the first scent you apprehend when smelling a perfume and will evaporate the fastest. The middle note will fade second, and the base note will linger on the skin after the perfume dries down. Just as the fragrance of essential oils can change when they are paired, a perfume can change on the skin dramatically over time from the opening burst of the top notes to the sultry, soft fade of the base notes.

We recommend using natural essential oils over fragrance oils that contain synthetic ingredients and additional carrier oils. Be sure to check if the essential oil is skin safe. When beginning, start small. Use only three to four essential oils to start and build up to a larger vocabulary.

This recipe creates a perfume oil—a "skin scent"—which hugs closer to the body and has a longer staying power than alcohol-based scents. The yield can be scaled up using the same ratios once your experimenting phase is complete and you have developed a perfume you truly love.

WHAT YOU'LL NEED

5 disposable pipettes

One 5-milliliter amber glass bottle

Perfume testing strips or coffee filters cut into ½-inch-wide strips

3 or more essential oils (at least 1 base note, 1 middle note, and 1 top note—see sidebar on page 132 on how to identify each)

4 milliliters carrier oil, such as jojoba or sweet almond oil

Adhesive labels

Makes 5 milliliters of perfume

DIRECTIONS

1. Wash and clean your pipettes and amber glass bottle.

2. Dip a test strip into each of your essential oils and allow to dry so you can test each scent.

3. Play with different combinations of the oils by holding different pairings of base, middle, and top notes together.

4. Once you have a group of essential oils that you like, use these ratios to help you determine proportions to mix. Keep in mind that 1 milliliter usually equals 20 drops of oil administered by pipette:

    2 parts base to 1 part middle to 1 part top

    40 percent concentration of essential oils to 60 percent concentration carrier oil

5. For a 5-milliliter recipe, this means that you will use 100 drops in total: 60 drops will be carrier oil, 20 drops will be base note, 10 drops will be middle note, and 10 drops will be top note. As you become more comfortable, play with the ratios to find a blend that suits you.

6. Start by adding your base note to the amber glass bottle, then the middle note, and finally the top note, smelling as you go.

7. Once your essential oils are mixed, label and date your mixture and allow the oils to marry for 2 weeks in a dark place.

8. Finally, add the carrier oil and allow the oils to marry in a dark place for 1 month. At the end of the month, the perfume will have coalesced and intensified and will now be ready to wear. Your perfume should last for at least a year if not more. The fragrance may change after that point, but will not spoil.

9. Dab lightly on pulse points for the most fragrant impact.

HOW TO DETERMINE BASE, MIDDLE, AND TOP NOTES

Fragrances are classified into three categories: base, middle, and top notes. Use this chart to help you navigate each scent and to blend the perfect harmony.

TOP NOTES

- **CITRUS:** For example, grapefruit, bergamot, mandarin, or neroli
- **SOME FLORALS:** For example, bright, green, and clean scents like lily of the valley, white flower, magnolia, etc.

MIDDLE NOTES

- **AROMATICS:** For example, rosemary, cumin, or lavender
- **CHYPRES:** For example, patchouli, oak moss, or labdanum
- **SOME FLORALS:** For example, jasmine, aldehyde, or rose

BASE NOTES

- **LEATHERS:** For example, smoke, tar, or animalic
- **ORIENTALS:** For example, vanilla, musk, or spice
- **WOODS:** For example, sandalwood, cedar, or cypress

Sweet

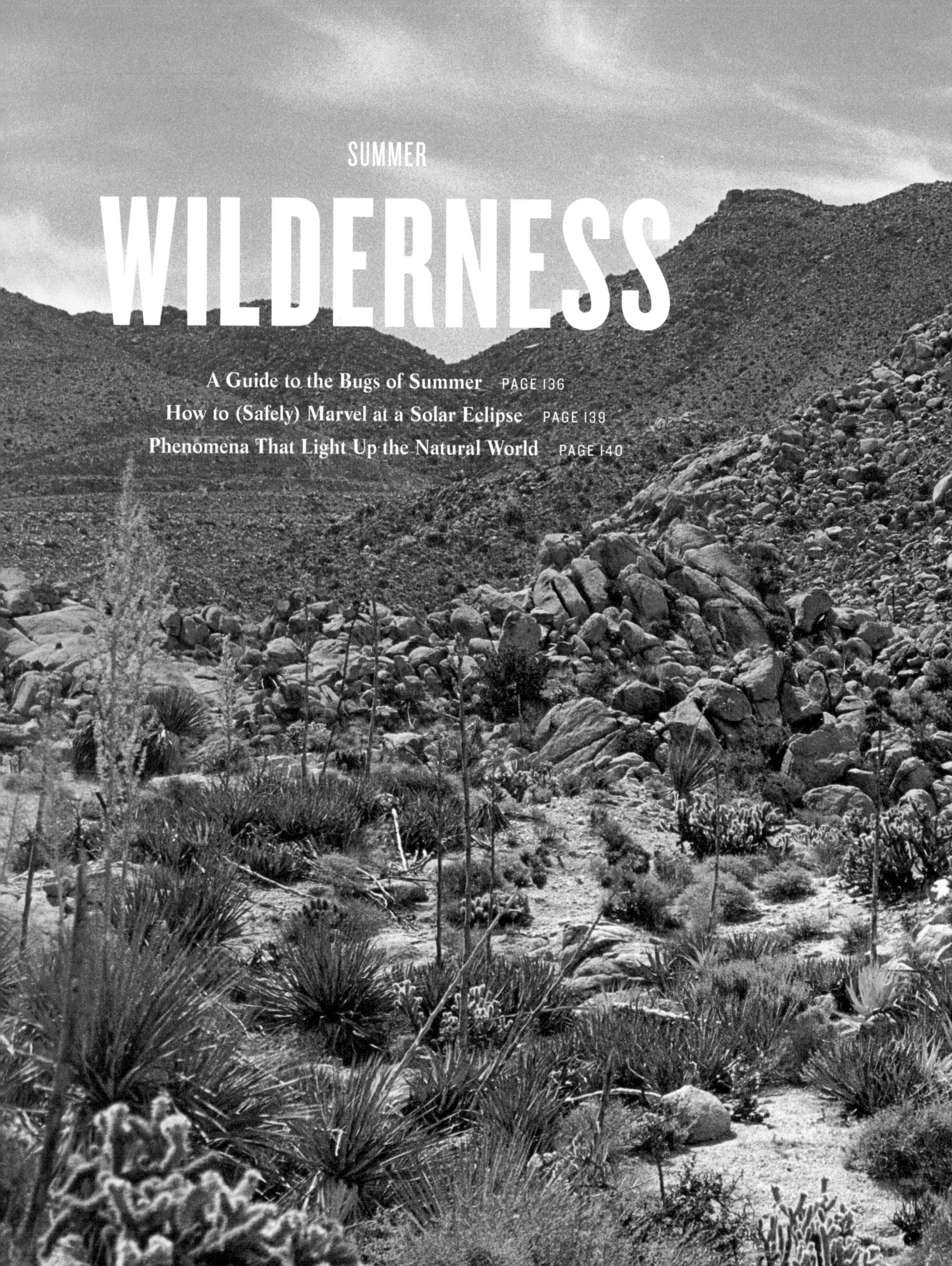

SUMMER

WILDERNESS

KNOWLEDGE

A GUIDE TO THE BUGS OF SUMMER

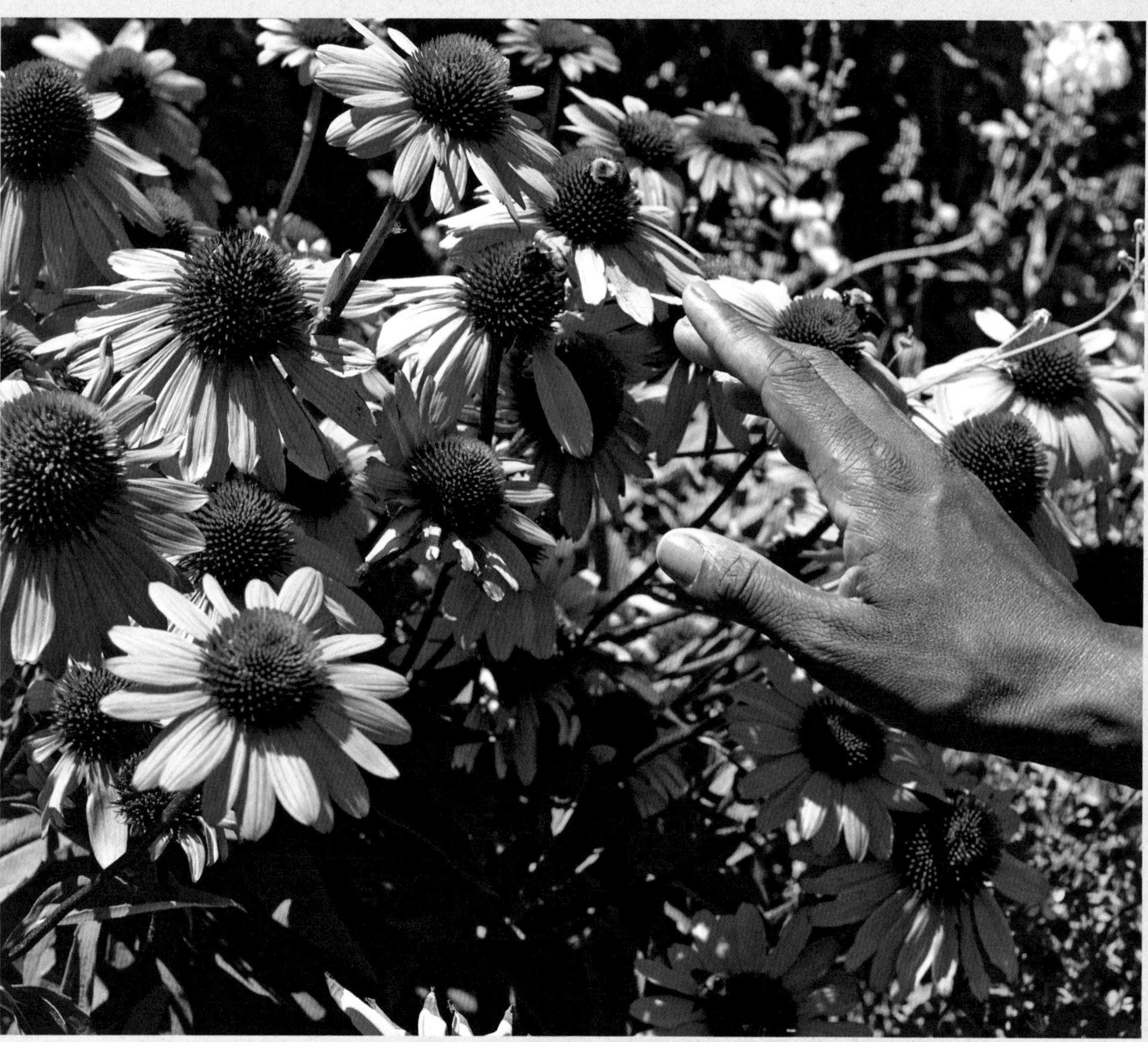

Be it the low buzz of a bee or the twinkle of a firefly, insects are the backdrop of the summer season. While various regions have their own special variety of summertime bug, there are stalwarts of the season we can all expect to see when the warm days of June come around.

BEES

The term "bumblebee" has come to be universal. In reality, all three bees—the honeybee, bumblebee, and solitary bee—have distinct identities.

Honeybees

There are seven species of honeybee with a total of forty-four subspecies, all of which produce the sweet treat of honey, but these bees are on the ropes. Over the last few years, there has been a lot of speculation about the decline of the honeybee, and most folks now agree that the main culprit in causing colony collapse disorder is pesticide. Do your part by limiting the use of chemical pesticides in your garden or window boxes.

Bumblebees

Bumblebees are the honeybee's kissing cousin. You can visually tell the difference between the pair, as the honeybee's stripes are generally gray, while bumblebees are color blocked with black and yellow and are fuzzy, to boot. Bumblebees live in the wild, floating from flower to flower, while honeybees are kept mostly by beekeepers. Bumblebees make very small amounts of honey, but their passion is pollination. These industrious bees are the backbone of a summertime ecosystem and can most likely be spotted working in your backyard garden.

Solitary Bees

Solitary bees are so named because they do not live in colonies like bumblebees or honeybees. They also do not create honey, but they are still excellent pollinators and therefore are essential to any garden or food farm. Varieties include the hornfaced, mason, and leaf-cutter bees. The latter cuts circles out of petals and leaves to build their nests in holes of wood or in tunnels in the ground. Solitary bees are picky creatures, choosing only a few plants to pollinate, unlike their cousins, who love all flowering plants equally.

CICADAS

There are over three thousand species of cicada living on almost every continent in the world. Due to their prevalence and size (cicadas can be as long as 7 centimeters with a wingspan of almost 20 centimeters), cicadas are more than just bugs. Many cultures have come to see the cicada as a symbol of reincarnation or immortality since they spend most of their lives underground as nymphs, only to emerge, molt, and take flight at the beginning of the summer season.

Cicadas are also known to "sing." In order to make their one-of-a kind song, male cicadas use their tymbal—a membranous part of the insect's exoskeleton—which contracts and expands to produce a clicking noise. The insect's hollow abdomen amplifies the sound creating the distinctive humming we've come to associate with the summer season.

FIREFLIES

With more than two thousand species, fireflies are the ambassadors of summer, with their bioluminescent mating call lighting up backyards and urban gardens.

It may seem like it would be easy to identify a firefly (the red, green, or yellow twinkle is a dead giveaway), but that doesn't take into consideration others that communicate via powerful pheromones, like the *Lampyris* genus, whose males emit no light at all.

Catching fireflies in a jar is a favorite summer pastime, but perhaps not for long. While the exact cause is unknown, fireflies are dwindling in number. One theory is that light pollution has substantially slowed their mating process. Male fireflies need to be able to see the female's winking response in order to know the game is afoot and mating is just a twinkle away. Overhead lights from crowded mini-malls or even lights reflecting off of low-slung clouds can distract or even blind them. Luckily, there is an easy fix. Turn off your outdoor house lights and let the fireflies light up the night.

GRASSHOPPERS

You can always tell when summer is coming to a close. That's when the gardener's great foe, the mighty grasshopper, appears. There are eleven thousand species of grasshopper, all of which possess powerful hind legs that enable them to leap distances as far as twenty times their body length. These insects are mostly herbivores feeding on urban garden staples like thyme and chives. Beware! Grasshoppers multiply in the blink of an eye, quickly becoming an out-of-control pest with the ability to decimate a garden.

If you're under attack from a gaggle of grasshoppers, here's a trick: feed them all-purpose flour. Using a saltshaker, gently dust your plants with flour (do not use self-rising). The flour will "gum up" the grasshoppers' mouths and essentially give them a bellyache, sparing your plants, while being completely eco-friendly.

YELLOW JACKETS

The yellow jacket is part of the feared wasp genera, sporting fierce stripes of yellow or white. While they seem ready to pick a fight, they're usually just looking for the sweet refuse from your picnic lunch. Yellow jackets are most dangerous near and around their nesting site. These are most often located in dense areas or in a burrow, making them hard to spot. Here's a tip: stand still and look. You can spot a nest by the handful of yellow jackets dipping in and out of a tree or the brush.

Despite their painful sting, yellow jackets are beneficial to humans—they feed pests such as flies and leaf-munching caterpillars to their young.

DIY

HOW TO (SAFELY) MARVEL AT A SOLAR ECLIPSE

Many of us share a common childhood memory—standing outside with our schoolmates gazing up through specially crafted glasses to catch a glimpse of our first solar eclipse. Also known as the "ring of fire," an eclipse happens when the moon comes between Earth and the sun during its orbit. It's a majestic sight and one that shouldn't be missed, but looking directly at a solar eclipse is incredibly dangerous. Your eyes dilate due to the low light levels. At the same time, ultraviolet light is still exuded around the eclipsed sun in what is called a corona, or halo, allowing UV light to escape, which could cause serious, permanent damage to your retinas. Never view an eclipse without using the proper equipment and technique. Thankfully, it's easy to make a pinhole projector to help shield your eyes from those dangerous UV rays, while still allowing you to capture one of nature's most incredible displays.

WHAT YOU'LL NEED

Shoebox

White paper

Scissors

Tape

Aluminum foil

Pencil

DIRECTIONS

1. If the inside bottom of the box isn't white, cut out a piece of white paper to the correct size and tape it to the bottom of the box.

2. Cut out two rectangles the length of the box top from opposite ends of the box. This will create two openings: one where you'll place foil and one through which you'll view the eclipse.

3. Tape aluminum foil over the left opening.

4. Use a pencil to poke a hole in the center of the foil. The size of the hole should be more than 2 inches but not more than 3 inches wide.

5. Stand with your back to the sun.

6. Hold the finished pinhole so that the sun's rays shine onto the foil with the pinhole.

7. Look through the right-hand side of the box for as long as you like—you are looking not at the sun, but at a refracted image. Move the image until the eclipsed sun appears at the bottom.

PHENOMENA THAT LIGHT UP THE NATURAL WORLD

One of the best things about camping is that you get to be cozy with nature. There's nothing quite like an evening surrounded by the smells, sounds, and sights that appear only once the sun has gone down. The night plays host to some of the most extraordinary and rarely witnessed phenomena nature has to offer. Look for these natural favorites.

Firefly Trees

Fireflies are one of our favorite insects. Their twinkling is not only romantic but also reminiscent of summer nights at sleepaway camp or the adult equivalent—drinks with friends alfresco on sweltering nights. A few fireflies are a treat. Hundreds, blinking as one, is a jaw-dropping spectacle. Across Southeast Asia and in a few spots in North America, including the Smoky Mountains, you can experience this mating ritual of the *Photinus carolinus* for yourself. This particular species of firefly often flashes in unison, but can flash in waves rolling across forests and hillsides that will take your breath away.

Bioluminescence

Bioluminescence, or living light, is the engine behind the fireflies that light up summer nights, but bioluminescence happens most impressively in the deepest corners of the ocean. In sunlit tropical waters, microscopic and planktonic single-celled dinoflagellates create magnificent light shows when disturbed, forming halos of blue-green light around swimmers and boats. When these organisms occur in great abundance, they create stunning bioluminescent bays, like the ones you'll find in Vieques, Puerto Rico. The deep sea is home to bizarre, alien-looking dragon fish and anglerfish with daggerlike teeth and bioluminescent lures and chin barbels, predatory glowing red siphonophores, luminescent starfish, comb jellyfish, squid, and even sharks that use bioluminescence to attract prey by making themselves appear deceptively smaller!

Foxfire

Foxfire is a rare natural nighttime phenomenon that lights up the corners of forests with its blue to bright-green light. Also known as "fairy fire," foxfire is caused by a range of bioluminescent fungi that feed on decaying wood. Its glow is powerful enough that it was used as a lantern in the Middle Ages and has been revered by everyone from Aristotle to H. P. Lovecraft, who immortalized the fungi in one of his poems. While it can be found in almost any forest, it is most prevalent in the tropics, as moist, damp fallen trees are its ideal environment. If you spot these mushrooms, don't hesitate to collect a sample. Foxfire makes an unusual tabletop arrangement that continues to glow for hours or even a few days.

Hessdalen Lights

Hessdalen is a small valley situated in central Norway. The county, measuring just under ten miles in size, is also home to the Hessdalen Lights. These flashing orbs have been appearing in the sky since the 1940s but remain unexplained—creating a fertile ground for UFO speculation. Other explanations include crystal formations or a "natural battery" of metallic minerals buried deep beneath the ground. While the science is still unclear, the majesty of the lights is undisputed.

Fall

PENTAX

FALL TENDS TO SNEAK UP ON YOU.

The heavy-lidded summer afternoons you've gotten used to now come through the door with a gusty, refreshing chill. And just as suddenly, the full Hunter's moon appears high above the night sky, telling you that dark mornings are soon to come.

Before your hibernation mode sets in, enjoy the bounty that is inherent to fall. Arugula, kale, leeks, tubers, squash, pears, apples, and pumpkins all become available in abundance at your local farmers' market or, hopefully, in your own garden or window boxes. Pair these autumn standards with offerings fresh from the nature around you. Take the time to get out of the city or the suburbs and head into the wild to forage for rarer delights such as mushrooms, nuts, wild grapes, and berries or Thanksgiving's star, the cranberry.

While the edibles are ready to be picked, the rest of nature begins to draw back inside itself. You'll notice the last gasp of some of your favorite summer blooms. And you'll find that the constant buzz of insects has faded away, and the songs of birds have become less frequent. Now is the time to prepare for next spring. Pinch back your plants. Select the bulbs you want to welcome you next growing season. Two of our favorites include the grape hyacinth, so very reminiscent of the fruit, and the extremely early spring riser, snowdrop.

Almost more than any other season, fall is meant to be enjoyed outside. The temperature is not so biting as during the frigid months of winter. And when you head outdoors, you won't be faced with torturous pollen, insects, or the heat that spring or summer can bring. Instead you'll find the great outdoors is on fire as green, lush leaves give way to a radical show of oranges, yellows, and reds (see page 196). The hot, muggy air of summer has mellowed and cooled, which means it's the perfect time for a hike; see page 194 for five of our favorites. Step off the beaten path and explore autumn while you can, for soon, winter's snow and ice will be at your door.

FALL

GROWING

FALL

A SEASONAL GROWING CHECKLIST

As the Earth pivots and slowly spins away from the sun, autumn arrives. Cooler, shorter days bring new haste to your chores in the garden, and every task—from planting and cleaning to gleaning—is done with winter's arrival in mind.

- ☐ **Lift and store tender bulbs and tubers, like dahlias and gladiolas.**
- ☐ **Plant winter vegetables in a cold frame.**
- ☐ **Divide crowded perennials.**
- ☐ **Store hummingbird feeders.**
- ☐ **Clean birdhouses.**
- ☐ **Plant new trees, shrubs, and perennials before the frost arrives.**
- ☐ **Rake leaves and make a leaf mold pile.**
- ☐ **Remove and throw away diseased foliage (don't compost).**
- ☐ **Collect seeds to be used again in the spring.**
- ☐ **Leave dead flower heads standing for winter birds and beneficial insects.**
- ☐ **Plant a cover crop, such as winter rye.**
- ☐ **Plant spring bulbs like crocus and fritillaria.**
- ☐ **Dig roots like escarole and rhubarb to force fresh shoots indoors over winter.**
- ☐ **Cure and store potatoes and onions.**
- ☐ **Pick blackberries, apples, and fall raspberries.**
- ☐ **Go mushroom hunting.**
- ☐ **Harvest and dry the season's last herbs.**

AMERICAN HOLLY

COMMON NAME

American holly

LATIN NAME

Ilex opaca

FRUIT TIME

Autumn through winter

LIGHT

Full sun to part shade

SOIL

Well-drained, acidic soil

PESTS & PROBLEMS

Tends to develop leaf spot; individual plants are either male or female

BEST USE

As an anchor or accent tree; excellent in woodland or wildlife gardens

There's something undeniably primitive and mysterious about the small, dark American holly—especially when it's brimming with bloodred fruits. Particularly conspicuous during the leafless months of its northern and eastern ranges, this evergreen tree creates an excellent habitat for overwintering birds and insects. The flowers, though small, are surprisingly sweet-smelling, too.

Seeds

The seeds benefit from immediate, direct sowing and will germinate under warm, moist conditions, generally the following spring.

Young Plants

Young plants must be planted in clusters to ensure that there is at least one male plant for every three females—otherwise, a good fruit set will not take place. The sex of young holly plants may not be discernible for ten years or more.

Mature Plants

Mature individuals require little care once established. However, the addition of acidic mulches such as bark or coffee grinds can be advantageous if growing the species in circumneutral soils. The species responds well to pruning and can be shaped into topiaries, formal hedges, or a single trunked tree to expose its beautiful, sinuous, smooth gray bark.

PLANT PROFILE

AUTUMN SAGE

To pick just one species of the expansive genus *Salvia* is needlessly restrictive. All members of the hardy, drought-tolerant group have a cherishable quality in common—they keep blooming when other flowers have already hunkered down for chilly weather. *Salvia greggii,* native to the Chihuahuan desert of Texas and Mexico, is one of the best autumn-flowering sages—its hot pink, maroon, and magenta flowers are excellent hummingbird attractants, and will make you believe that winter will never come.

Seeds

Cold-stratified seeds will readily germinate in spring. If you're collecting home-grown seeds, harvest the seed capsules when they're dry, but not yet open. Allow the capsules to burst on newspaper in order to catch all the minuscule seeds. Store the seeds in a sealed bag in the refrigerator, or directly sow in a prepared garden bed.

Young Plants

Young plants will take a year or two to bloom. Keep watered and free from weeds until well established, to encourage good growth and development.

Mature Plants

Mature individuals require little water or care once established. After the first flush of flowers, deadhead the plant to encourage more buds. Both the flowers and the leaves of autumn sage can be collected and brewed into a refreshing, slightly minty tea.

COMMON NAME

Sage

LATIN NAME

Salvia greggii

BLOOM TIME

Late summer through autumn

LIGHT

Sun

SOIL

Moist, rich, neutral soil

PESTS & PROBLEMS

Cannot tolerate wet soils or extreme cold

BEST USE

In rockeries and difficult, drought-prone areas

UNDERSTANDING THE PROPERTIES OF SOIL

Soil provides the building blocks that all plants need to grow and comes in a kaleidoscopic array of types. In reality, the rich dark soils, alive with microbial activity that most gardeners dream of, are not easy to come by. Fortunately, adding compost or lime will quickly fix most problems, but there is an easier way out: there are more than enough plants to fit the multitude of naturally occurring soils—it just takes knowing which type of soil your garden has.

The first tool in the soil-savvy gardener's kit is a simple pH test. A good vegetable or cut-flower garden should have circumneutral soil, around the 6.5 pH mark. Anything lower than 6 is known as acidic, and anything higher than 7 is known as *basic*. The organic content present in soil also greatly influences what can and can't be grown in it. Although soil's pH can give some indication of its organic content, this characteristic can be quickly assessed on site by squeezing a small handful of it: dark soil that clumps together in small, loosely formed clods indicates plenty of organic matter, while soil that sticks together tightly or does not clump at all is a sign of its overly rich clay content or lack of essential nutrients, respectively. A soil's draining capacity will also influence planting plans. Dark, rich, crumbly soil retains and drains water moderately and is known as *freely draining*. Soils heavy with clays, or frequently saturated with water, will often appear bluish to yellow in color and do not drain well. Almost all soil ailments can be fixed with the addition of compost. Increased organic matter allows for better aeration, drainage, and can adjust pH levels, too.

SOIL FIRST AID

An easy alternative to amending your garden's soil is finding plants that are suited to grow in it naturally. If your soil is sandy, grow drought-tolerant plants or flowers that colonize old meadows and roadsides. For clay or silt-rich soil, choose plants that don't mind a lot of moisture, like those seen in swamps, bogs, or wet seeps. Look for native options at your favorite nursery; they're often more tolerant of a wide range of naturally occurring soils.

TYPE OF SOIL: Sandy

COLOR: Medium to very pale brown

TEXTURE: Loose, very fine

WATER RETENTION: Low

GROW: Milkweed, succulents, rosemary, lavender

TYPE OF SOIL: Clay

COLOR: Yellowish to blue and red

TEXTURE: Easily clumps together

WATER RETENTION: High

GROW: Ironweed, cana lily, false indigo, coneflower

TYPE OF SOIL: Loam

COLOR: Dark, rich brown

TEXTURE: Crumbly

WATER RETENTION: Medium

GROW: All common garden cut flowers and vegetables

SKILL

BE PICKY AND SAVE SEEDS

Great potential lurks within the hull of every seed. Mostly, plants cross-pollinate, reproduce, and continue to beautifully adapt themselves to the vagaries of the environment. Every once in a while, however, a truly magnificent mutation occurs, bringing gardeners brighter color, bigger blooms, or longer flowering time. Saving the seeds of excellent performers ensures that their offspring will carry on the show. Learn to store those propagules properly and next season you can sow the seeds of success, quite literally, across the garden.

WHAT YOU'LL NEED

Notebook

X-Acto knife

Muslin bags

Paper bags or envelopes

Labels

Seeds

DIRECTIONS

1. Keep a notebook. As spring and summer advance, keep track of eye-catching blooms or appealing oddities in the garden. Plants that bloom first, produce prolific quantities of flowers, or last longer than the rest carry a desirable set of genes. Blossoms that all of a sudden emerge sporting stripes or surprising colors may have an interesting mutation worth cultivating and preserving for future seasons.

2. Know the collecting season. Spring ephemerals set seed as early as May. Nut trees are ripe and ready as late as December. Late summer is the busiest season for seed collection when new buds seem to turn from flower to fruit in the blink of an eye.

3. Pick at just the right time, when mature seeds are full and fat. Juvenile seeds won't grow if picked too early. Sacrifice one seed from your collection, making an exploratory incision with an X-Acto knife. The endosperm—or inside of the seed—should be full and white, or pale green. Empty or withered hulls and signs of insect frass are sufficient cause to throw seeds away. Hint: many berries change color as they ripen—red often signals seed maturity.

4. If the seeds look mature, harvest more than necessary. Place all seeds directly in a muslin bag or a paper envelope to keep dry. Fungi, next to insects, are the number one seed predators. They are almost completely invisible and thrive in moist environments. Assume a portion of your seeds will be lost while in storage and gather 25 percent more than is needed for your garden. Add a label to each collection detailing the species name, and when, where, and why it was collected.

5. Seed storage needs vary. While some seeds require cold stratification—a certain number of weeks at cool temperatures—others do better if sown right away. Generally, a breathable paper bag tucked away in a cool, dry cupboard will satisfy the demands of many temperate species. A good rule of thumb is to keep seeds at approximately 50 degrees Fahrenheit and less than 50 percent humidity. If in doubt, store them in the fridge, but not in the freezer.

6. Don't forget your seed collections; they will not last. Although some seeds remain viable for decades, most decline rapidly after the first year. Freshly collected seeds are best sown the following spring before fungi, and time, get the chance to do their dirty work. For instructions on planting your seeds, see page 26.

SKILL

HOW TO FORCE VEGETABLES IN THE FALL

Even on the darkest, coldest days of the year, fresh vegetables can be grown indoors with ease. The age-old technique known as "forcing" works best on rhubarb, chicory, and the cabbagelike sea kale. Gradually sapping their roots of summer energy storage, forced plants will grow only for two to three months, and must be discarded at the end of winter. For the fast version of forcing, throw a handful of dried beans in a Mason jar full of water and soak for eight to ten hours. Drain the water and set in a warm, dark cupboard for three to five days until sprouts appear. These quickly grown fresh sprouts can be thrown into stir-fries or salads.

WHAT YOU'LL NEED

Root crowns of plants to be forced

Sharp knife

An opaque pail or bucket

Sand

Potting soil

Lid for bucket

DIRECTIONS

1. Dig up the fattened roots of rhubarb, chicory, or sea kale at the end of the summer.

2. Using a sharp knife, cut off any remnant foliage close to the root crown, and pack the roots tightly together in a bucket.

3. Add an almost even ratio of loose damp sand and potting soil to the bucket and tamp down using your fingertips to make sure all air spaces are closed. The soil should be level with the top of the roots, leaving the crown, or point of growth, exposed. Close the bucket with the lid.

4. Place the bucket in a dark cupboard or basement and make sure the temperature stays in the 50° to 70°F range. Water frequently enough to keep the soil moist but not dripping.

5. Harvest the edible shoots every three weeks until the plants are no longer productive. Compost exhausted roots, or plant in the garden come spring—perhaps a little rest and relaxation will bring them back.

FALL

COOKING

FALL

INGREDIENTS TO INSPIRE

Fruits

APPLES

ASIAN PEARS

CACTUS PEARS

CHESTNUTS

CLEMENTINES

DATES

FIGS

GRAPES

MELONS

NECTARINES

OLIVES

PEACHES

PEARS

PERSIMMONS

PLUMS

QUINCE

Vegetables

ARUGULA

BEANS

BEETS

BLACK SALSIFY

BROCCOLI

BRUSSELS SPROUTS

CABBAGE

CARROTS

CAULIFLOWER

CELERY

COLLARDS

DAIKON RADISH

EGGPLANT

GARLIC

GINGER

GOURDS

HOPS

JERUSALEM ARTICHOKE

KALE

KOHLRABI

LEEKS

LETTUCE

ONIONS

PEAS

PEPPERS

POTATOES

PUMPKINS

RADICCHIO

SPINACH

SUMMER SQUASH

SWEET CORN

SWEET POTATOES

SWISS CHARD

TURNIPS

WINTER SQUASH
(ACORN SQUASH, BUTTERNUT, KABOOCHA, DELICATA SQUASH)

ZUCCHINI

KNOWLEDGE

PANTRY ESSENTIALS

Just as important as knowing what vegetables to use at the height of each season is knowing what to stock year-round in your pantry. Aside from the normal stash of dry pasta, rice, flour, and sugar, there are key extras to keep in your cupboard. Here are our go-to ingredients to enhance your dishes and give depth of flavor to your favorite meals any time of year.

ALMOND MEAL: A little thicker than almond flour, almond meal is shelf-stable and can be used as a bit of crumble on top of pasta dishes, a thickener in Spanish-style soups, or an unexpected flavor in breading for chicken.

ANCHOVIES: This polarizing fish—people either love it or hate it—can be a miracle-worker when incorporated into salad dressings and sauces to give an added layer of briny umami.

ARBORIO RICE: Often overlooked and simple to make any day of the week, arborio rice can be transformed into a luscious and satisfying risotto with just a little help from soup stock and whatever odds and ends happen to be in the fridge. Don't underestimate this humble grain.

BAKING SPICES: Stick to the classics and build from there: cinnamon, nutmeg, allspice, clove, and ground ginger are useful in myriad baked goods. Cardamom, mace, star anise, and vanilla bean will take your dishes to the next level.

BALSAMIC VINEGAR: The longer this vinegar has been aged, the more mellow and rich the flavor. Whether it's a mature or a young variety, this richly hued condiment gives brightness and tartness to salads, stews, and even desserts that feature strawberries or chocolate.

BLACKSTRAP MOLASSES: This particular type of molasses is created from the third boiling of raw sugarcane and thus contains the lowest amount of sucrose. It does, however, contain vitamin B_6, as well as calcium, iron, and magnesium. Use this black, sticky beauty for baking and in marinades where a touch of sweetness is desired.

CHILI SAUCE: Sriracha or chili garlic sauce options will give heat to any dish, regardless of the country of origin, but marry particularly well with East Asian flavors.

COARSE KOSHER SALT: Take note when recipes call for kosher salt instead of table salt. Coarse kosher salt's large flakes are less dense than table salt's individual grains; the two are not interchangeable. Chefs prefer to use kosher salt for cooking because it is easier to handle and easier to distribute onto dishes. Plus, it has not been treated with additional chemicals or minerals.

DRIED KOMBU: Add this dried seaweed to soup stocks to reap the benefits of iodine and minerals found in the sea, not to mention its flavor.

DRY LENTILS, BEANS, AND GRAINS: We love watching while cannellini, black, or adzuki beans plump up with a little water and become silky, creamy, and nourishing. Keeping dried beans on hand will ensure that a hearty soup is never far from reach.

FISH SAUCE: Most often described as "funky" smelling, pungent fish sauce is essential for capturing the Southeast Asian flavors found in Thai or Vietnamese cooking. Its flavor can range from rich and salty to almost nutty, and will add deep umami to marinades, soups, sauces, stir-fries, and noodles.

GOOD-QUALITY OLIVE OIL: Considering that this will be the first ingredient in almost everything you cook, make sure you like its flavor. Like all things that grow in the ground, olives will vary in taste based on where they are grown. Taste different olive oils and find the one that suits your palate.

HERBS AND SPICES: Before winter sets in, trim your fresh herbs like rosemary, thyme, sage, and mint. Grind them up using a well-cleaned coffee grinder and store for year-round use. Pony up for good-quality spice blends like Indian garam masala and curry, Chinese five-spice, and Middle Eastern za'atar.

HOMEMADE SOUP STOCK: A lovely and cost-effective habit to start: when you cook, save your vegetable scraps like carrot ends, onion skins and tops, and celery trimmings to slow cook and turn into stocks that can become the base for a future soup or stew. These "small batch" stocks can be frozen individually for later use.

HONEY: Good for everything from pancakes to sore throats, keep honey on hand to add natural sweetness to most anything.

KAFFIR LIME LEAVES, DRIED: You can't always have a fresh lime in the fridge, but you can keep these dried leaves on hand. Create aromatic, floral citrus notes in soups, noodle dishes, desserts, and marinades without a zester by adding these miraculous dried leaves. The same goes for dried lemon verbena.

MALDON SEA SALT FLAKES: A home cook's secret weapon is this salt. Essential? No. Indispensable? Absolutely. These crunchy, salty, pyramid-shaped flakes should be sprinkled onto your plated dishes or your baked goods before they go into the oven to add a spectacular burst of flavor.

POWDERED MILK: We've adopted Milk Bar chef Christina Tosi's philosophy about powered milk. No longer the vestigial remnant of 1950s bomb shelters, powdered milk has been reborn with new purpose: adding a caramel-y, ineffable flavor to baked goods. Use it as Tosi does to bring an extra-gooey, cozy taste to sweet treats.

RICE VINEGAR: Made from fermented rice or rice wine, this acidic yet sweet elixir can be used to brine vegetables, make salad dressings, or create fruity, distinctive marinades.

TAMARI: This is the liquid by-product of miso as it ferments. Unlike its ubiquitous relative, soy sauce, which can be made anywhere, tamari is exclusively made in the Chubu region of Japan and is said to be closest to the original version of soy sauce that was brought from Japan to China. Tamari is usually made without wheat and is darker and richer in flavor than soy sauce but can be used interchangeably to add umami flavors and saltiness.

TOMATO PASTE: Tomato paste is an absolutely essential ingredient for creating a depth of flavor in stews, tomato sauces, soups, and roast meat dishes.

WHOLE-GRAIN MUSTARD: A staple of continental European cooking, whole-grain mustard adds complexity—salinity, spice, heat, and acid—to just about anything it meets.

RECIPE

MAKE PUMPKIN BUTTER

Nothing seems quite as iconically autumnal or soul warming as a bite of pumpkin pie. You can make the most of the seasonal good vibes by capturing that beloved pumpkin essence with pumpkin butter. Unlike jams and jellies, fruit butters don't rely on terrific amounts of sugar to make them set, nor pectin to make them firm. This type of luscious spread is the fruit, pure and simple, cooked down to remove the water, lightly sweetened, and seasoned to taste. Because of this, canning fruit butters can be challenging; we prefer to freeze our pumpkin butter in small containers for individual use—if there is any left over, that is.

Though store-bought pumpkin can work for this recipe, we prefer to roast our own pumpkins for the happy by-product of roasted pumpkin seeds and for the fresher flavor. Look for sugar pumpkins or pie pumpkins, and opt for smaller fruits. The larger pumpkins can be not as sweet and tougher to work with. This recipe calls for twenty-eight ounces, which will be your approximate yield from two small pumpkins. If you have any leftover puree, freeze it for later use. It will keep frozen for up to six months.

Spread pumpkin butter on brown bread or muffins, but the spiced wonder can also be an interesting addition to baked goods in place of regular butter or even in stews where the pumpkin will provide a rich texture and depth of flavor.

INGREDIENTS

28 ounces pumpkin puree (from 2 small, fresh pie pumpkins or one 28-ounce can)

¾ cup apple juice, homemade or store-bought

½ cup brown sugar

2 tablespoons honey

2 tablespoons molasses

1 tablespoon cinnamon

1¼ tablespoon cloves

¼ tablespoon allspice

1 tablespoon ginger

EQUIPMENT

Baking sheet

Food processor

Saucepan

Plastic containers or ziplock freezer bags

Makes 1 quart

DIRECTIONS

1. To make the pumpkin puree, lop off the top stems of both pumpkins and cut the pumpkin bodies into quarters. Scoop out the seeds and reserve them. (You can roast them on a baking sheet, then toss them with olive oil and salt, and use them as a snack or salad topper.)

2. Heat your oven to 400°F. Place the pumpkin quarters on a baking sheet and roast for 60 minutes or until the pumpkin is soft to the touch and a knife can easy be inserted.

3. Once the pumpkin is roasted, remove the outer skin using a knife or your fingers—it should peel away.

4. Place the pumpkin in a food processor and mix until blended. It should resemble the consistency of baby food.

5. Measure out 28 ounces of the pumpkin. Place any remaining pumpkin in a plastic ziplock bag and freeze for later use.

6. Place the pumpkin puree, apple juice, and brown sugar in a saucepan and cook over medium heat.

7. Cook for 30 minutes, stirring occasionally, being careful to not let the pumpkin burn.

8. Add the honey, molasses, and spices and cook for another 30 minutes, stirring occasionally. When the mixture has darkened and thickened into a loose paste, the pumpkin butter is done.

9. Transfer the mixture into airtight plastic containers or freezer bags. The pumpkin butter will keep for 1 week in the fridge or several months in the freezer.

FALL

HOME & SELF-RELIANCE

FALL

PREPARE YOUR HOME FOR THE SEASON

Fall is the time to shutter the windows and prepare for the cold and rainy season ahead. Some areas of the country will experience the bountiful harvest that extends well into deep autumn, so this is the time to stock your pantry. As temperatures drop, make sure both you and your home have enough insulation. Unpack extra blankets and sweaters to save on your heating bill and to keep you toasty as cooler weather sets in.

- ☐ **Insulate windows with storm windows or plastic to keep the heat inside.**
- ☐ **Put up end-of-harvest fruits and vegetables (see page 100 for a primer on canning).**
- ☐ **Protect all doorways from drafts with doorstops or rolled blankets.**
- ☐ **Move potted plants indoors for the cold season.**
- ☐ **Switch bedding to warmer blankets and down comforters.**
- ☐ **Create hanging planters for indoor plants (see page 179 for instructions).**
- ☐ **Grains are harvested in the fall; stock up now for the freshest crops.**
- ☐ **Clean any sweaters, coats, or jackets that have been in storage.**
- ☐ **Collect kindling for the woodstove.**
- ☐ **Stack all chopped wood in a dry location.**
- ☐ **Hang out hibernation boxes for bees and other beneficial insects.**
- ☐ **Clean out gutters in preparation for more rain and snow.**
- ☐ **Ripen late fruit on the windowsill or in paper bags.**
- ☐ **If raising chickens for eggs, install a bright, full-spectrum lamp inside the coop to keep up egg production.**
- ☐ **Add straw or shavings to a chicken run to make sure wet ground doesn't turn to mud.**
- ☐ **Use the fall harvest to make pumpkin butter (see page 167).**
- ☐ **Gather fallen leaves for the compost pile.**
- ☐ **Get a head start on cold weather projects like knitting, weaving (see page 52), or mending.**

HEAT AND COOL YOUR HOME WITHOUT ELECTRICITY

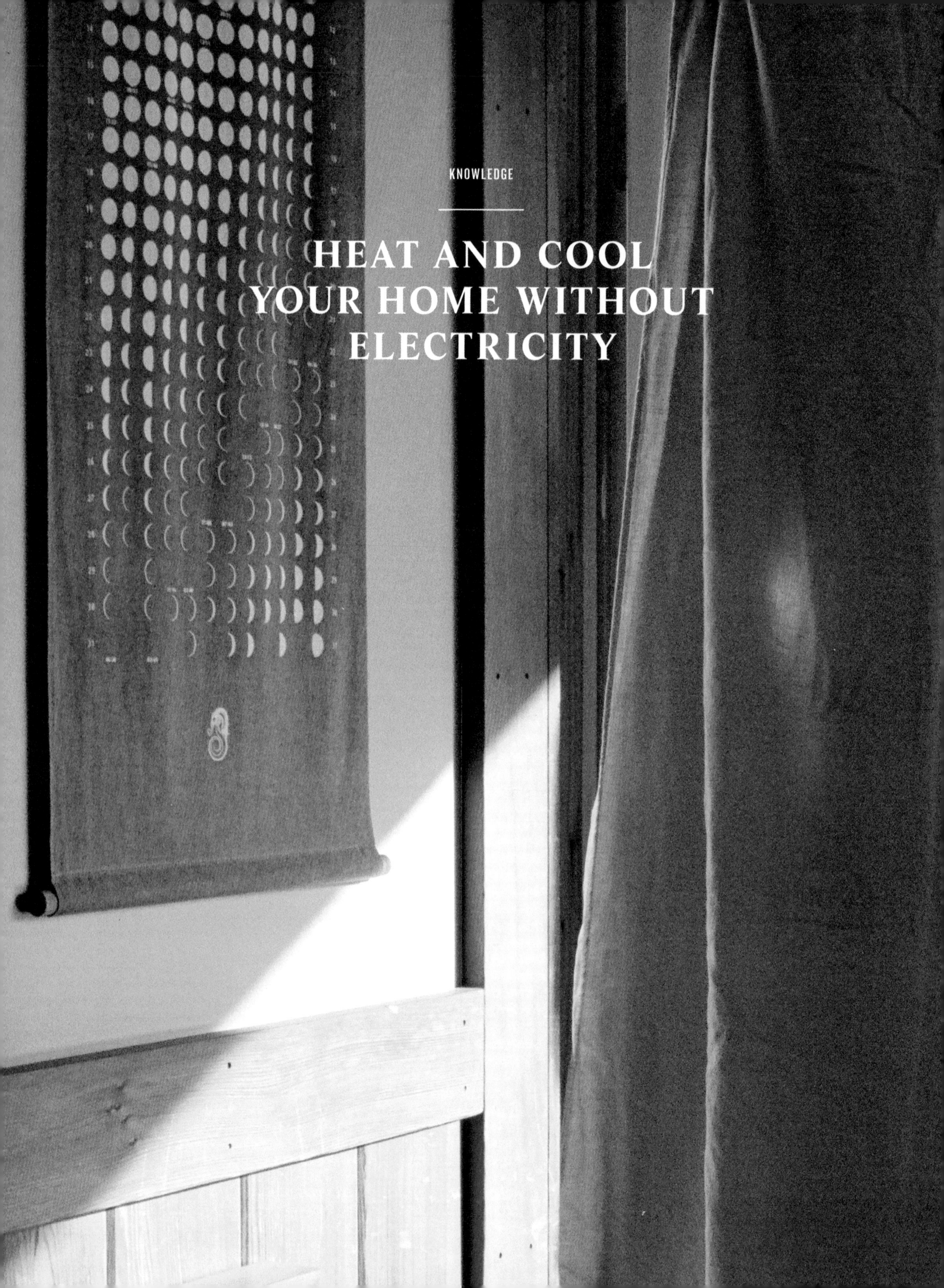

Heating and cooling your home can be expensive. But beyond the expense, home heating and cooling has a notable impact on the environment. According to the U.S. Department of Energy, in the United States, over a half billion tons of carbon dioxide are emitted into the atmosphere every year by heating and cooling systems. In addition, they generate 24 percent of the national average of sulfur dioxide emissions. Combined, these two gasses are significantly contributing to global warming. Cooling systems, in particular, tax our power resources. On hot summer days, air conditioner energy consumption accounts for 43 percent of the nation's power usage.

Thankfully, we have a great asset available to us free of charge: the sun. Passive solar energy design uses the sun's natural rotation to heat and cool interior spaces. In these designs, buildings and their surrounding environments become temperature regulators, passively maintaining a controlled temperature—as opposed to active systems, which use natural gas or electricity for regulation. With passive solar heating, natural processes like conduction, convection, reflection, radiation, and insulation are used to harness the sun's heat to create a uniform, livable indoor temperature. With a few simple tricks, you can limit your dependence on home heating and cooling systems—without installing major solar collectors or alternative energy mechanisms. Here are some tips to show you how.

HEATING YOUR HOME

When the temperature dips, our thermostat temperatures rise, giving way to high heating bills and dry, stuffy air. Though stale indoor air can be mitigated with the use of houseplants, temperature regulation is key. Using the following methods and considerations will help you keep warm without turning up the thermostat.

House Orientation and Window Placement

In the Northern hemisphere, where heat is the most pressing concern, homes that face south will receive the most benefit from the sun's rays in the winter. If building or buying a home, make sure there are enough south-facing windows to be able to let the sun's light in. If renovating an existing home, ensure that there are opportunities to create those windows.

Solar Gain Space

The key to passive solar heating is trapping the heat that enters a space. South-facing windows are important, but containing the heat that comes through them is the real name of the game. An adequate solar gain space made from thick concrete, brick, or stone, or having a large quantity of heatable thermal mass (a tiled floor, say) in view of south-facing windows, will warm up during the day when the sun's rays are active, absorbing the heat and preventing the home from becoming too hot. At night, the heat will rise and warm the home even after the sun has set. Follow this passive solar design rule of thumb: one cubic foot of thermal mass per square foot of solar visibility.

Insulation

Once your home has been heated, make sure none of that heat escapes. Fit or retrofit walls, windows, and doors with caulk and insulation to keep heat indoors. Opt for triple-paned windows, which can retain heat three times better than a single-paned window.

COOLING YOUR HOME

Many of the considerations for heating your home go into cooling it, too. Shade and protection are of vital importance; and once the ideal temperature is achieved, insulation also keeps cooler air from escaping.

Reflecting the Heat

In areas of extreme year-round heat, opt for light-colored surfaces on your home's exterior that can reflect sunlight instead of absorbing it. Homeowners and remodelers should paint their homes' exterior a bright, light color to keep it cool. By contrast, dark-colored surfaces can absorb up to 80 percent of the sun's rays, trapping heat and warming interior spaces.

Blocking the Heat

Protect your home from the sun's rays by incorporating shaded areas and landscaping trees and shrubs. Green roofs that modulate temperatures and provide a buffer zone can be a great option. As with heating the home, insulation will protect interior spaces from changing temperatures outdoors; begin with the attic where hot air is often trapped.

Cross Ventilation

Opening windows across from one another and allowing cool air in at night can be a great way to naturally lower the temperature in your home. Investigate regional and seasonal wind patterns to better understand how to make the most of natural ventilation.

Heat-Generating Activity

Save heat-generating activities like drying clothes, baking, and boiling hot water until the evening when the sun has set and it has become cooler outdoors. The heat produced by these activities in combination with excessive daytime outdoor temperatures will make indoor temperatures even hotter.

Though larger projects like solar panels and green roofs can also contribute to the overall heating and cooling effect of your home and limit dependence on energy sources further, these simple acts—from planting a tree to opening a window—can still have a dramatic effect on your year-end energy bill. Start small; you'll be amazed at what the little steps can do.

KNOWLEDGE

AN INTRODUCTION TO PLANT-BASED CEREMONIES

The use of plants in ceremonies and rituals in the home or sacred spaces has a history almost as varied and long as humanity itself. From spiritual beliefs, ritualistic practices, and the healing arts, to recreational use, plants and herbs have been burned, imbibed, distilled, and worshiped in the name of a higher purpose.

You need not be an expert to try incorporating some of these plants and herbs into your home life. You'd be surprised what bringing small rituals like attentively making a cup of tea or ritualistically burning incense can do to connect you with a moment of quiet and with nature. Below is a list of our favorite ceremonial plants and herbs. For information on herbs' medicinal properties, see page 184.

Agarwood and Sandalwood

These highly resinous, highly aromatic woods are made into incense in Japan and burned during a traditional incense ceremony, or as a preparation for meditation, tea ceremony, calligraphy, or ikebana, the Japanese floral art. Kyara, an incredibly rare and potent variety of agarwood, is said to be worth more than its weight in gold.

Cedar

In Native American traditions, cedar is burned while prayers are offered both silently and aloud. It is said that the smoke of the burned cedar will carry these wishes and prayers into the sky and to the creator.

Matcha

Made from the ground leaves of *Camellia sinensis*, this powdered green tea is used as the basis for Japanese tea ceremonies, a meditative act that follows a prescribed order of motions and aesthetics for preparing and drinking tea. The detailed process allows the practitioner to focus solely on the preparation of the tea, which is said to bring about a serene, contemplative state.

Peyote

Used in North American ceremonies for thousands of years, the small cactus *Lophophora williamsii* from which peyote is derived, contains psychoactive alkaloids like mescaline, which create a deeply introspective and hallucinogenic effect—the ideal mind-state for entering into meditation ceremonies.

Sweet Grass

This calming grass is harvested in late summer. In some Northern European Christian traditions, sweet grass was strewn at the entrances to churches on saints' days. When people would enter the church and walk on it, the sweet grass would emit a subtle perfume into the air, lending sensual appeal to the ceremony.

In Native American traditions, sweet grass is braided, dried, and then burned in peace ceremonies and healing rituals. The faintly vanilla-scented fragrance is said to put the mind in a state ready for meditation and also to remind one of his or her connection to the earth.

Tulsi (Holy Basil)

In Ayurvedic and Hindu traditions, tulsi is regarded as the holiest of plants. It is grown outside the entrances to healers' homes to prevent evil spirits from entering, as well as in many orthodox Hindu homes where it is often worshiped and occasionally worn. Ritualistic care of the tulsi plant by watering and making offerings is said to cleanse the worshiper and bring perfect health. Tulsi is also incorporated as a culinary herb and steeped and imbibed as a medicinal tea.

White Sage

Sage is the most common herb used in smudge ceremonies in Native American cultures. For the cleansing ritual, a smudge stick is created principally by bundling dried sage and binding it with string or twine—though other herbs are also used in some cultures. The smudge stick is then burned with focus and attention to cleanse a person or the environment and drive out bad spirits, emotions, or influences. The smudge stick is also burned as a precautionary measure to keep bad spirits from entering a place.

HOW TO MAKE A MODERN MACRAMÉ HANGING PLANTER

Macramé has gotten a bad rap over the years. Originally developed as a way to finish weavings in ancient Babylonia, the knot-tying technique became a favorite of sailors who spread the art form throughout the world on their travels. The Victorian era favored macramé for making tablecloths, curtains, and delicate, lacy wearables. In the 1970s, macramé knots were used to create elaborate wall hangings and belts, and the 1990s saw hemp macramé jewelry for neo-hippies, grunge kids, and frat boys alike. Suffice to say, macramé has seen its fair share of style changes, and yet it still endures.

In part, this is because it is so easy to do. If you can tie your shoelaces, you can make this planter. It relies on two traditional macramé knots, the square knot and the overhand knot, which you may recognize as knots you use in a variety of everyday tasks.

In the square knot, the right outermost strand is brought to the left side and the left outermost strand is crossed in front of the right strand and brought to the left side so that the two strands have changed positions and looped through each other.

In the overhand knot, a loop is formed with a pair of strands and the end is brought through the loop. This is the type of knot you would use to secure the end of the thread in sewing.

Once you've nailed these simple knots, more complex macramé knots can be substituted in the same proportions in the pattern below. Or, go wild and create your own pattern—macramé offers endless variations and with just a little practice you can master them all.

WHAT YOU'LL NEED

72 feet of cord, made of cotton, hemp, or nylon

4-inch metal ring

Scissors

Glue

Potted indoor plant

DIRECTIONS

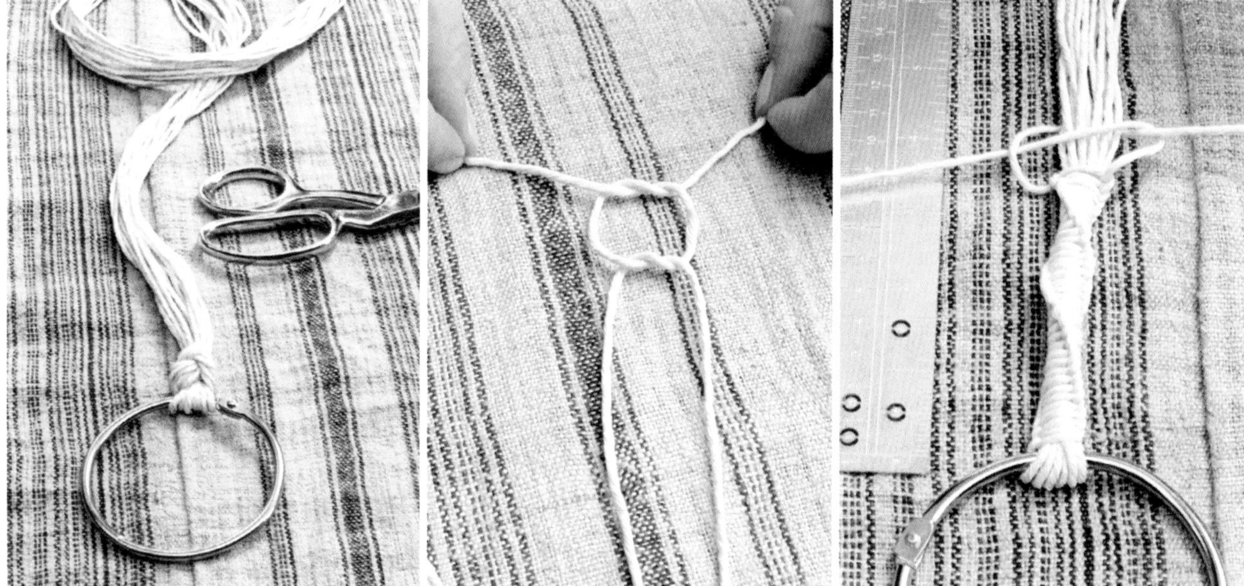

1. Temporarily attach your metal ring to a nail in the wall, a chair, or a table to create tension while you tie your knots.

2. Cut the cord into four 18-foot pieces and place them through your metal ring.

3. Pull each piece of cord halfway through the metal ring. You will now have eight pieces of cord; make sure that all the ends are the same length.

4. Take the two outermost pieces of cord and separate them from the group of cords.

5. Using the outermost pieces as your working strands, create 6 inches of square knots, tying the outermost pieces around the inner six remaining pieces.

6. Divide the group of cords into four pairs. Then tie a knot in each pair 18 inches down from your square knots column (see photo).

7. Take the left cord from a pair and tie it to the right cord of the pair next to it using an overhand knot (see photo). Repeat for all pairs.

8. Measure 4 inches down and repeat the previous step.

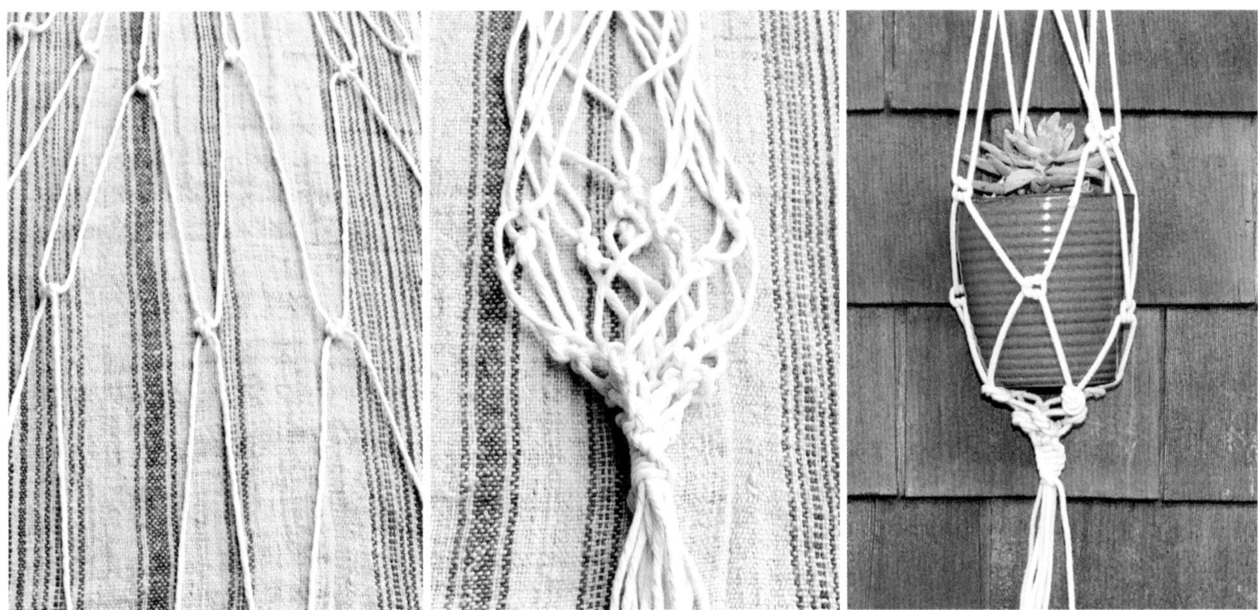

9. Measure 3 inches down and repeat the previous step.

10. Measure 2 inches down and repeat the previous step.

11. Join all the cords together, and using the same method you used for your first column, tie 2 inches of square knots using the two outermost cords to tie around the inner 6 cords.

12. Secure your final knots with glue and allow to dry overnight.

13. Cut the excess tassel to the desired length.

14. Suspend your planter from the ceiling and place your plant inside its new home.

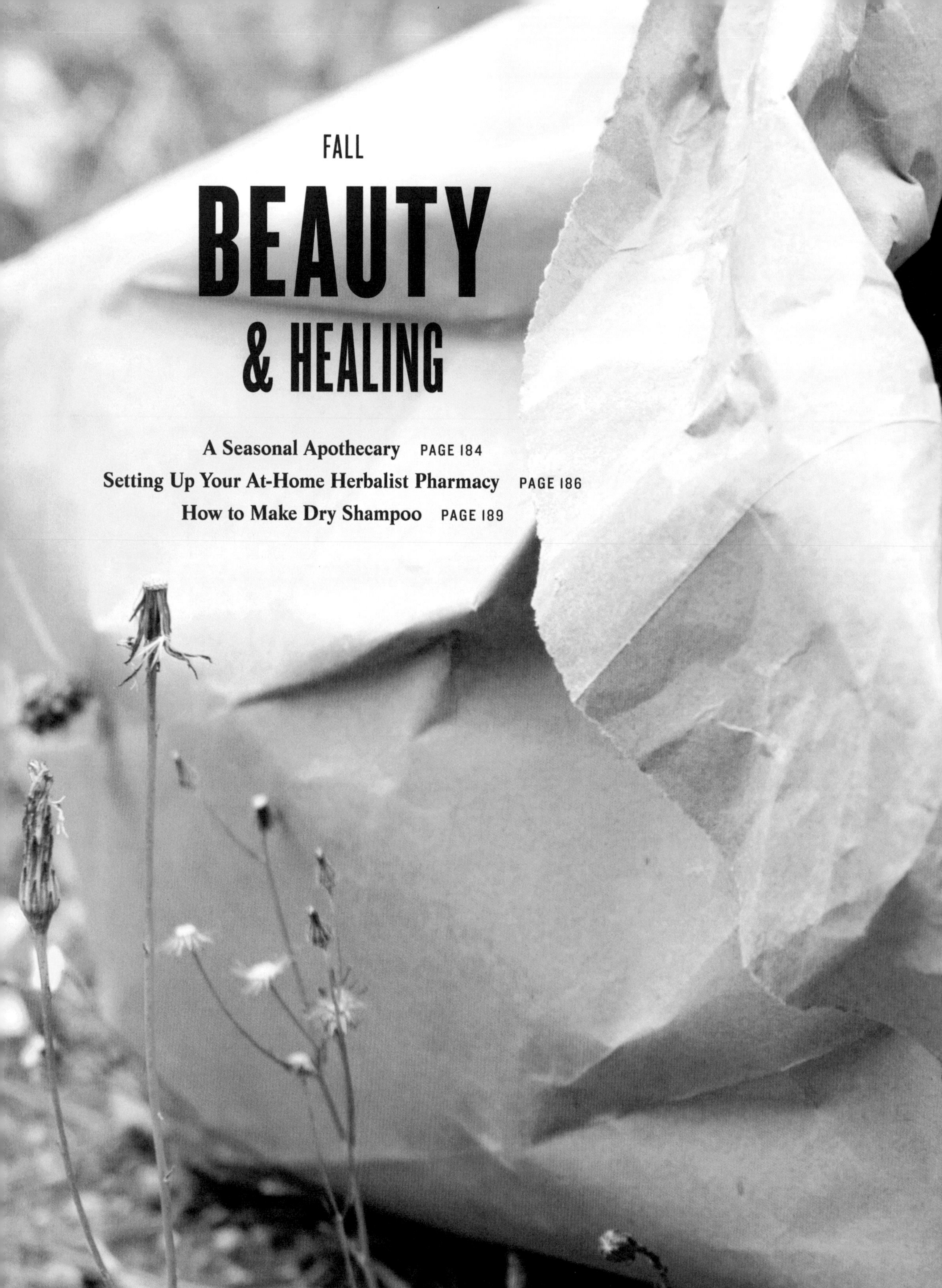

FALL

BEAUTY & HEALING

KNOWLEDGE

A SEASONAL APOTHECARY

The first chill of fall can seem sudden after so many days spent in the lavish summer sun. The typical cold and flu season can be brutal during the fall, as can first bouts of dry skin. Reach for warming herbs and spices like cinnamon and turmeric to help your body adjust to the shock of cold or rain. Some, like valerian, can help balance your system in this shift of seasons. Check the spice aisle at your local grocery store to find more common spices and herbs. For resources, see page 265.

HERBS TO IMPROVE VITAL FUNCTIONS

Valerian
Helps sooth anxiety, tension, and insomnia. Use the root to make a tincture or tea.

Eucalyptus
An excellent aid for respiratory discomfort. Use as an essential oil in a hot bath or as a salve.

HERBS TO SOOTHE DRY SKIN

Calendula
The ultimate herb for treating dry, chapped, or irritated skin. Use as a salve (see page 252 for recipe).

HERBS TO COMBAT SICKNESS	HERBS TO WARM UP AND COMFORT THE INSIDES
 **Echinacea** Known to boost the immune system for combating infection during the early stages of an illness. Use as a tincture.	 **Cinnamon** Warms the body and improves circulation. Use as a culinary herb, in honey or tea, or as a tincture.
 **Goldenseal** Traditionally used for fighting infections, colds, and flus that have already set in. Use as a tincture—it's very bitter!	 **Turmeric** Warming to the digestive system and stimulating to the immune system. Use as a culinary herb.
 **Licorice** Soothes irritated and inflamed tissue; widely used for treatment of cough or sore throat. Use the root to make a tea.	
 **Marsh Mallow** Demulcent, lubricating, and moisturizing; marsh mallow is excellent as a cough suppressant and throat soother. Use the root to make a tea.	

KNOWLEDGE

SETTING UP YOUR AT-HOME HERBALIST PHARMACY

Modern medicine is a marvel. We've cured diseases, performed microsurgeries to reconnect human tissue, cloned a sheep, and—on the more banal level—developed medicines to combat irksome colds. But sometimes even the best cold medicines can't compare to a steaming hot cup of tea with honey and lemon, when a sore throat starts to bother you. At the root of all medicine—or at least at the beginning of all medicine—lies nature. After all, before aspirin was a staple on every drugstore shelf, it went by a different name, acetylsalicylic acid, most commonly found in willow bark extract. Reference to its anti-inflammatory and fever-reducing properties can be found as early as Hippocrates' writing in 400 BCE.

In addition to natural aspirin, we have all most likely used some form of an herbalist's treatment. From chamomile tea to aid in relaxation, to valerian root for a good night's rest, the beneficial uses of herbs are all around us. But setting up an at-home natural pharmacy goes beyond store-bought tea or herbal supplements. You can use fresh and dried herbs in a variety of preparations to partake in the goodness of nature. You can easily make these preparations at home; here are a few of our favorites. Use this information to prepare your plants and herbs for medicinal use.

DECOCTION: A decoction is similar to a tea but instead uses hard plant matter, such as roots, rhizomes, stems, and bark. Allow the plant matter to rehydrate overnight in a pan filled with water. In the morning, simmer the mixture over medium heat for twenty to thirty minutes and strain. Sip as you would a tea.

HERBAL BATH: An herbal bath soothes body aches and skin irritations. Steep plant matter as you would a tea, using four tablespoons or more of plant matter and one quart of hot water. Steep for twenty minutes, strain, and add to bathwater.

HERB OIL: Herb oil is an effective topical or ingested treatment. Combine two parts olive oil to one part plant matter in a glass jar and let steep for two to four weeks. Strain the oil, through a sieve lined with cheesecloth. Squeeze the cheesecloth to make sure all excess oil is extracted from the plant matter. The oil can be applied directly to the skin and massaged in to receive the benefits of the herbs transdermally. It can also be used as a cooking oil or in salad dressings. Store for up to one year.

SALVE: A salve combines herb oils with beeswax to form a silky topical treatment for skin irritations, burns, dry skin, and other ailments. For our favorite recipe—Calming Calendula Balm—see page 252.

TEA OR INFUSION: A tea or an infusion is made by a process of steeping herbs, flowers, and seeds in boiling water and allowing the water to permeate the plant matter. Fresh or dried plants can be used. For dried, use one to three teaspoons of plant matter per cup of water. For fresh plants, double the amount.

TINCTURE: A tincture is similar to an infusion, but in place of water, alcohol, glycerin, or vinegar is used to extract the beneficial properties of the herbs. Our favorite way to make a tincture: Fill a glass jar with plant matter, leaving one inch of space. Then fill the jar with 100-proof alcohol (vodka or brandy works well). Seal it and allow the jar to rest in a light-free closet or cupboard for two to six weeks. Strain the liquid and then administer in drops either directly on the tongue or in a cup of tea or juice as needed.

KITCHEN TOOLS FOR YOUR AT-HOME PHARMACY

You probably have many of the tools necessary for making herbalist treatments in your home already. Herbalism relies on foundational knowledge of plants and minimal equipment, so the tools needed are neither expensive nor fancy. Though not much has changed in the way of herbalist logic in the past five thousand years, the addition of some modern electric appliances, such as an herb grinder, simplifies the process of making decoctions and salves at home. Here is a list of tools every herbalist should have.

Adhesive labels for naming and dating your remedies

Airtight glass jars (amber or light-protected glass works best)

Blender (for fresh plant matter)

Cheesecloth

Coffee grinder (to be used exclusively for dried herbs)

Fine-mesh sieve

Funnel

Glass vial and eyedropper

Permanent markers

Scissors

Sharp knife and cutting board

Spatula

Stainless-steel pan

HOW TO MAKE DRY SHAMPOO

Dry shampoo is a game changer. It has altered the styling—and, ahem, bathing—habits of many. And with good reason. This wonder potion has been known to preserve a good hair day even after a night's rest, and lend extra volume—and even intoxicating scents—to greasy, flattened locks. But commercial dry shampoo formulations often include additives and chemicals that are far less appealing, such as silicon dioxide, a chemical suspected to be a carcinogen.

This recipe is for a plant-based alternative that has the added benefit of doubling as a natural perfume. Superfine arrowroot powder is harvested from the rhizome of the perennial herb *Maranta arundinacea* (or arrowroot) and tapioca starch is derived from cassava root (*Manihot esculenta*). Rich in trace minerals, medicinal montmorillonite clay is added to the mix to help absorb excess oil from the scalp. These ingredients combine to create a very fine powder that you can apply to dry hair either by hand or with a brush or comb for styling options without any nasty side effects.

EQUIPMENT

Glass mixing bowl

Whisk

Tea towel

Spice shaker or airtight container

3 teaspoons arrowroot powder

WHAT YOU'LL NEED

2 teaspoons tapioca starch

1 teaspoon montmorillonite clay powder

25 drops essential oil

Makes 1 ounce

DIRECTIONS

1. Place the arrowroot, tapioca, and clay powder in the glass mixing bowl and whisk together.

2. Select your essential oils. If mixing multiple oils, combine them to achieve the right balance first (see page 131 for how to blend your own perfume).

3. Slowly add the essential oil to your powder mixture, whisking continuously. Sprinkle the drops around the bowl; do not add them all in the same spot. The powder will absorb the oil, so keep mixing until you have a fine powder with a consistent texture.

4. Cover the mixture with a tea towel or other lightweight cloth to allow the ingredients to marry overnight and to ensure that the essential oils are completely absorbed by the powders.

5. Transfer the powder to a spice shaker or an airtight container and use by sprinkling on dry hair when needed.

6. The mixture will keep for up to one year.

WILDERNESS

FIVE HIKES OF A LIFETIME

Any season is great for hiking, but fall especially has so much to offer. Cool air, the colors of the changing leaves, and the smells of the season—damp earth, decaying flowers, fresh mushrooms—will immediately connect you to nature. Here are five of our favorite hikes that feature autumn in all its glory.

CALIFORNIA: THE LOST COAST TRAIL

While building the legendary Route 101, the highway that runs along the Pacific Coast, the State of California bypassed a section in Humboldt and Mendocino counties, due to its extremely rugged terrain. This decision led to almost seventy thousand acres, known as the Lost Coast, being preserved for your enjoyment. Named the King Range National Conservation Area, this stretch contains eighty miles of jaw-dropping hiking trails featuring black sand beaches and gorgeous mountain peaks. One of the most magnificent trails is the Lost Coast Trail.

Tips for Hiking the Lost Coast Trail

- This trail is of moderate difficulty. Great for hikers in good shape.
- We suggest a minimum of three days for the full hike, but stunning portions can be done in a full day. Check with the park for more details.
- Many parts of this trail are ocean side and unsafe during high tide, so time your hike accordingly.

JAPAN: THE NAKASENDO TRAIL

During feudal times, the Nakasendo Trail was a major trade thoroughfare between Kyoto and Tokyo. This three-hundred-plus-mile-long road is beloved as it brings hikers in close contact with the countryside. En route, you'll see traditional hotels and restaurants in small, refurbished towns such as Tsumago and Kiso-Fukushima. You'll cross rice paddies and trek through forests beside legendary mountains.

Tips for Hiking the Nakasendo Trail

- Easy for all ages.
- The main trek takes four to five days to complete. There are numerous companies, groups, and guides available to help you navigate the trail. One suggestion is Walk Japan at www.walkjapan.com.
- Beware! English is not spoken in the smaller towns. Either book reservations before arriving with the help of a native speaker, hire a guide, or bring along a translation app such as Google Translate.

MAINE: THE CADILLAC MOUNTAIN NORTH RIDGE TRAIL

Acadia National Park has more than 120 miles of trails, but one route—the Cadillac Mountain North Ridge Trail—is a stunner. This might be the most perfect place for you to see the sun rise in the United States, since Cadillac Mountain is the highest point on the Atlantic coastline. From its peak, you'll be able to enjoy the panoramic view, which includes the Cranberry Isles, Bar Island, and the Schoodic Peninsula. It's a fast four miles to the top, but you might want to dawdle all the way down the three-mile return, since the back half of the trail offers freshwater ponds, statuesque spruce trees, and a variety of peacefully swaying grasses.

Tips for Hiking the Cadillac Mountain North Ridge Trail

- Moderate difficulty.
- A great hike for bird-watching.
- Waiting for the sunrise on an autumn morning can get chilly. Bring along a thermos and blanket to make things cozier.

NEPAL: POON HILL

Trekking in Nepal is an obvious choice. The area is home to eight of the ten highest summits and some of the most beautiful landscapes in the world. For day hikers, take on the family-friendly five-day Poon Hill trek. The trail is popular, so don't expect solitude. What you will find is spectacular scenery along a trail that winds through villages and lush forests to the top of Poon Hill. The downhill trek takes you through one of the largest fields of rhododendron in the world.

Tips for Hiking to Poon Hill

- You can take this trek on our own or hire a guide. Try Original Trails at www.originaltrails.com.
- The morning trek up Poon Hill to catch the sunrise can get overcrowded. Look for the stone marker offering an alternative path up the mountain.

NEW YORK: LOWER GREAT RANGE LOOP

Set in the Adirondack Mountains, the Lower Great Range Loop is just a short three- to four-hour drive from New York City. The roughly seventeen-mile hike takes you past some of the best sites any upstate mountain range has to offer. This classic hike is demanding, but well worth the effort, as it traverses all five of the range's four-thousand-foot peaks: Sawteeth, Gothics, Armstrong, Upper Wolfjaw, and Lower Wolfjaw.

Tips for Hiking the Lower Great Range Loop

- This is a challenging hike. Prepare to break a sweat.
- Get out on the trail early, as this is a full-day hike.

KNOWLEDGE

THE SECRETS OF FALL'S CHANGING LEAVES

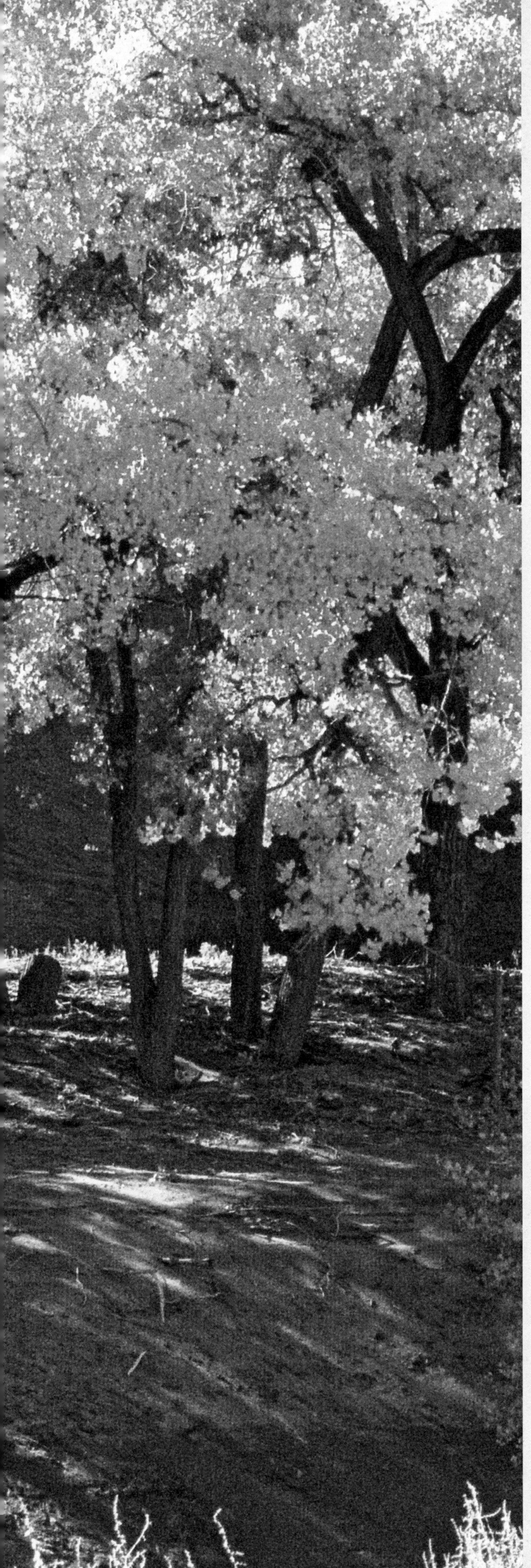

There is nothing quite like a tree's slowly shifting display of color, from the rich greens of summertime to the oranges, reds, and dusty browns of fall. Have you ever wondered just what causes this miraculous shift in palette?

During the summer months, the leaves of a tree are doing the heavy lifting—engaging in round after round of photosynthesis. As you might recall from grade school, this is the process by which a plant converts water and carbon dioxide into energy. The active ingredient in this recipe is chlorophyll, a pigment that gives a tree's summer leaves that rich green hue.

As the nights get longer, the air gets colder and fall begins to assert itself. Winter is coming and with drier air and shorter hours of direct sunlight, photosynthesis won't be possible for a tree. And so the tree stops producing chlorophyll and seals off each leaf with a layer of corklike cells.

That's when carotene and xanthophyll come into play. These two pigments help a plant absorb sunlight and are always present in the leaves. But with chlorophyll out of the way, they get their chance to shine. Carotene, from the Latin for carrot, gives us the stunning array of orange leaves that we see in the fall months. Trees such as sumac, dogwood, and sweet gum are carotene carriers. Xanthophyll, from the Greek *xanthos*, which means yellow, is responsible for leaves of saffron, maize, and gold. The pigment responsible for the vibrant red of the season is called anthocyanin—produced in response to the bright light of the autumn sun and excess sugars within the leaf. Hickory, ash, beech, and aspen are rich with anthocyanins.

While this process happens every year, the brilliance of the season is determined by the weather in early autumn. If it is dry and sunny when the chlorophyll is beginning to wane inside the leaves, expect to see more reds since those conditions increase the amount of sugar concentration in a tree. In cooler and cloudier autumns, you can expect to see more yellows and oranges appearing in the leaves, since sugar production will be at a low point.

Once the colors begin to fade and turn to brown, you know that the separation layer between leaves and chlorophyll is complete—the leaves have been completely cut off from the tree and will begin to fall to the ground. Winter has arrived.

SKILL

HOW TO BUILD AN OUTDOOR SHELTER

Human beings have four basic survival needs: food, water, shelter, and fire. While some might argue the order of importance in a true survival situation, shelter is paramount. Always remember the rule of threes: a person can last three minutes without oxygen, three hours without heat, three days without water, and three weeks without food. One way to make it through a chilly night outdoors is with the help of a debris shelter. It's the only makeshift shelter that will keep you warm on spring nights without the presence of a fire.

To build a debris hut, search for a sturdy stick to act as a ridgepole; it should be three to four inches in diameter and ten to twelve feet long. Lash one end of the pole to a tree, at hip height, using rope, large leaves, or an unused piece of clothing, or place one end of the pole in a natural tree fork.

Next, lean pieces of wood a bit longer than your ridgepole and about as thick as your wrist against the ridgepole. Allow about eight inches of space on either side of where your prone body will be. Place a thin layer of light brush against the ribs of the structure, then pile on the debris to create thermal mass. This layer should ultimately be at least two feet thick. Alternate between light brush and leaves when necessary.

Stuff the inside of the shelter with the driest material available, creating a soft bedding of leaves. Voilà, you've made a debris shelter.

Winter

WINTER IS KNOWN FOR ITS BITTER-COLD TEMPERATURES AND A RELUCTANT, SLUGGISH SUN.

Those unwelcoming characteristics often make us want to stay indoors, viewing winter's wonders from behind windows instead of venturing out. While it may appear to be quiet, not all of nature is asleep during winter.

Step outside on a dark early morning and you can hear the subtle sounds of winter and find its rare, beautiful growth. Stand still, hold your breath, and peer into nature to find its hidden treasure. You'll see icicles forming, and the swishing and swirling of water caught in a whirlpool. Ponds flood and brooks swell with abundant rain and snow. Berries flame red amid slate-gray woods. And there are more shades of green in the landscape than words to describe them.

Even those who love the wintertime may find it a challenge to keep their spirits up by the end of the season. For the beaten-down or merely cold-averse, winter presents itself as the perfect season for making things. From decorative moss balls (page 216) to delicious, pungent kimchi (page 231), there are hundreds of projects to occupy your time while you're waiting for the snow to melt.

Remember, without the cold nights of winter, you won't truly enjoy and appreciate spring, so explore the season while it lasts.

GROWING

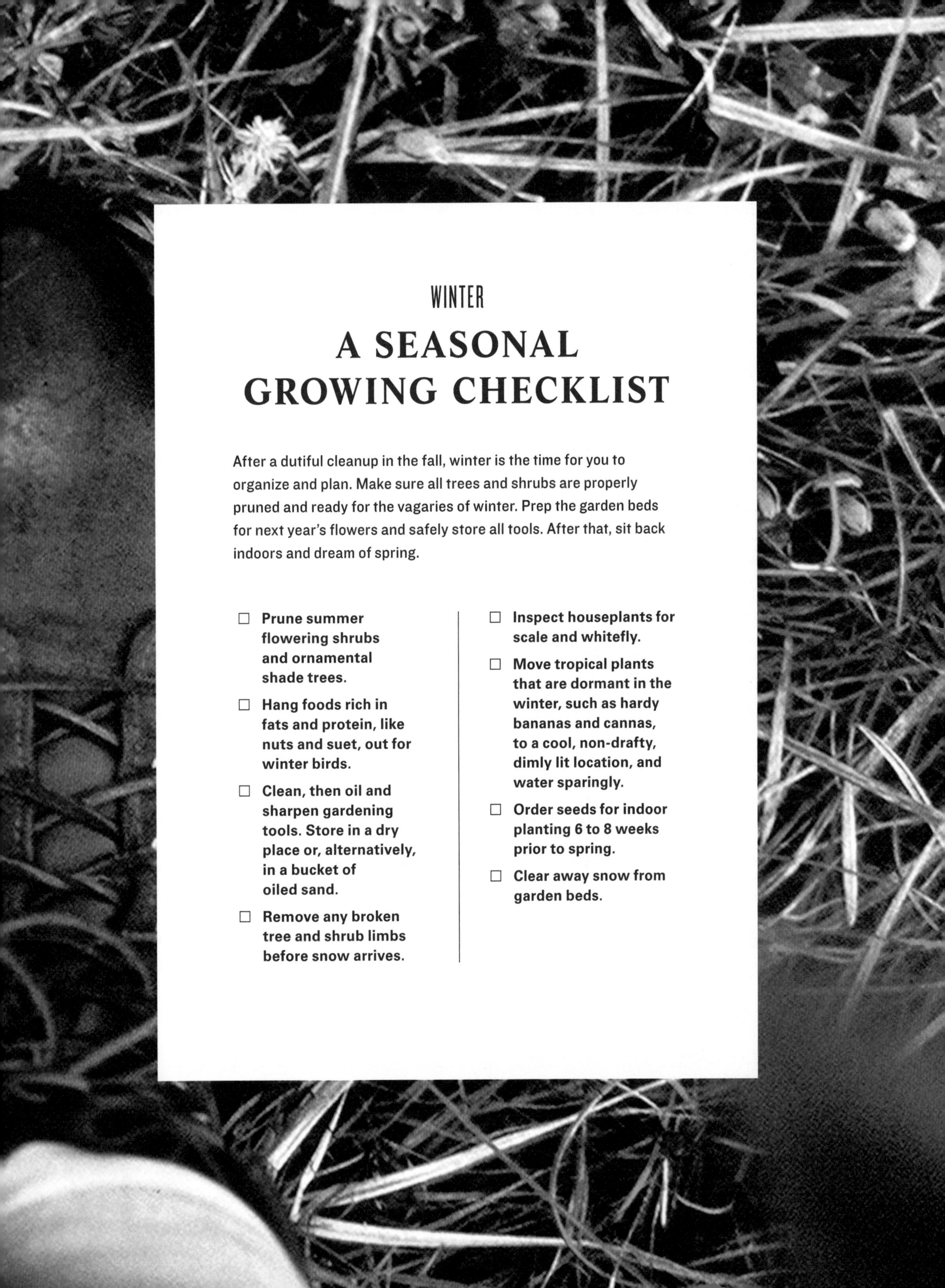

WINTER

A SEASONAL GROWING CHECKLIST

After a dutiful cleanup in the fall, winter is the time for you to organize and plan. Make sure all trees and shrubs are properly pruned and ready for the vagaries of winter. Prep the garden beds for next year's flowers and safely store all tools. After that, sit back indoors and dream of spring.

- ☐ **Prune summer flowering shrubs and ornamental shade trees.**
- ☐ **Hang foods rich in fats and protein, like nuts and suet, out for winter birds.**
- ☐ **Clean, then oil and sharpen gardening tools. Store in a dry place or, alternatively, in a bucket of oiled sand.**
- ☐ **Remove any broken tree and shrub limbs before snow arrives.**
- ☐ **Inspect houseplants for scale and whitefly.**
- ☐ **Move tropical plants that are dormant in the winter, such as hardy bananas and cannas, to a cool, non-drafty, dimly lit location, and water sparingly.**
- ☐ **Order seeds for indoor planting 6 to 8 weeks prior to spring.**
- ☐ **Clear away snow from garden beds.**

COMMON NAME
Camellia

LATIN NAME
Camellia

BLOOM TIME
Autumn to early spring

LIGHT
Part sun

SOIL
Acidic, rich, freely draining soil

PESTS & PROBLEMS
Camellia blight and canker; spider mites in hot, dry weather

BEST USE
Dense thickets in partially shaded garden areas

PLANT PROFILE

CAMELLIA

A modern symbol of enduring love and haute couture, the camellia is the belle of the winter garden. Found wild everywhere from the Himalayas to Indonesia, the plant has hundreds of cultivars that have evolved over the years, and many medicinal properties. It makes a sweet oil useful in cooking, and a tea is brewed from the leaves of one species. Relatively easy to maintain, these striking dark and glossy shrubs can be grown by almost anyone. Camellias prefer rich, acidic soils and need plenty of water. Their grand, fleshy flowers range in color from deepest magenta to delicate white and although largely scentless, are as seductive as any rose.

Seeds

Although fresh seeds readily germinate, they may not produce the same plant the seeds were collected from. When seedlings are two to three inches high, transfer them to individual pots.

Cuttings

Cuttings are an easy way to propagate favored camellia varieties. Cut in midsummer and root in a well-misted, freely draining mixture of peat moss and coarse sand.

Young Plants

Water young plants well and pinch back shoots to encourage branching. Keep temperatures cool—between 35 degrees and 65 degrees Fahrenheit.

Mature Plants

Plant camellias in partial shade in slightly acidic, well-drained, rich soils. Prune in winter after flowering.

PLANT PROFILE

PERUVIAN QUEEN

Native to the mild, mountainous climate of tropical South America, Peruvian queen is the perfect indoor plant. In the wild, it enters dormancy to avoid heat and drought, and flowers after the first rains fall. At home, the plant will do the same: let it slumber through hot summer, and it will light up your house with colorful blossoms at the darkest time of the year.

Bulbs

Peruvian queen is grown quickly and easily from bulbs. Bury the bulb with its neck barely exposed in a one- to five-gallon pot and fill with a freely draining soil mix high in organic material. Place in a brightly lit area indoors and keep the soil moist.

Young Plants

Once shoots begin to emerge, feed and water the plant regularly. Peruvian queen bulbs must be about the size of a baseball before they can flower and may require some time to reach maturity.

Mature Plants

Mature Peruvian queens prefer well-lit, warm areas that mimic the bright and mild conditions of their tropical mountain homes. To bring the plant into bloom, force dormancy by stopping watering and feeding altogether for two months. Flowering will occur approximately eight weeks after regular watering and feeding has resumed.

COMMON NAME

Peruvian queen lily

LATIN NAME

Phaedranassa dubia

BLOOM TIME

Winter

LIGHT

Full to part sun

SOIL

Rich, freely draining soil

PESTS & PROBLEMS

Dislikes excessive heat or cold

BEST USE

Potted indoor plant

KNOWLEDGE

CHOOSING A TREE

Trees are the backbone of every garden. They draw the eye, command attention, provide shade and habitat, and will outlast all other plants by decades. Choosing a tree requires an evaluation of the proposed planting site's natural characteristics such as soil type, sun exposure, available moisture, and the intended function of the tree. Fortunately, there is a wide variety of trees to choose from, so you have a good chance of finding one that will do well in your preferred location. You may also want to select a tree for its blossom, fruit, value to wildlife, fall color, or more practical characteristics like its ability to provide protection from wind or prevent soil erosion.

Trees planted outdoors should be hardy and able to withstand the weather they will encounter. Fall and spring are good times to plant trees as the cool weather and rain give saplings time to grow roots before hot weather arrives. If planting in spring, remember to water new trees consistently throughout the summer.

For indoor trees, light and water are often the biggest challenges. Make sure new trees are not stressed by watching for yellowing leaves. Indoor trees have a big root system squeezed into a small pot, so always water once the soil dries out and feed during the summer growing months.

Whether it will be indoors or outside, the tree you choose should have an unblemished, straight trunk. A trunk with scars or crooked growth may indicate damage or disease. If selecting a tree during summer, look for bright, glossy foliage with no sign of spots, bubbles, or discoloration on the leaves. A healthy tree will have a full crown of leaves or, if purchased in any other season, sizeable, fat buds. Base the size of your new tree on how many people you have to help plant it. Digging a hole for anything much bigger than four feet tall is very hard work to do on your own. To determine just how large that hole will need to be, a good rule of thumb is that the width should be at least three times the diameter of the tree's root ball or container.

TRIPLE-THREAT TREES

These trees are arboriculture favorites and triple threats: each one either bears fruit, has a beautiful blossom, or provides habitat for birds and other wildlife. They are true standouts in an otherwise quiet winter garden.

AMERICAN PERSIMMON (*Diospyros virginiana*)
At the beginning of winter, the orange fruits of the American persimmon begin to ripen and then hang like orange baubles throughout the season.

BIGLEAF MAGNOLIA (*Magnolia macrophylla*)
This large magnolia has some of the biggest leaves of any tree.

DESERT WILLOW (*Chilopsis linearis*)
Another choice for arid, sunny locations, Desert willow is an excellent hummingbird and pollinator attractant.

LACEBARK PINE (*Pinus bungeana*)
Beyond creating year-round habitat for birds, this pine also has gorgeous piebald bark.

MANZANITA (*Arctostaphylos manzanita*)
This tree is virtually unbeatable for creating a wildlife habitat. It offers shelter, as well as food sources, and a place for animals, such as squirrels, to nest their young. Manzanita is a very easy tree to care for, especially in dry places.

MEXICAN ELDERBERRY (*Sambucus mexicana*)
This large shrub grows to treelike proportions and has attractive dusky blue berries suitable for both wildlife and humans.

PAWPAW (*Asimina triloba*)
Otherwise known as a custard apple, it bears large, creamy, delicious fruits at the end of summer.

JAPANESE SNOWBELL (*Styrax japonica*)
In late spring, the snowbell dangles delicate powder-white bells from its graceful, arcing branches.

KENTUCKY YELLOWWOOD (*Cladrastris kentukea*)
Blooming in spring, yellowwood has beautiful racemes of white flowers and silver bark that seems to glow in winter.

YOSHINO CHERRY (*Prunus x yedoensis*)
The queen of blooming trees in early spring, Yoshino cherry puts on a prolific display of lush, pale pink blossoms.

KNOWLEDGE

GROW A WINTER GARDEN

As days shorten and temperatures slowly fall, your activity in the garden will start to dwindle. Although the flowers essential for fruit come to the end of their blooming season, the onset of winter doesn't mean your garden has to stop working entirely. With a little advance planning, and ample protection from colder temperatures, you can enjoy leafy greens like kale, mizuna, and arugula even while the snows blow and frost forms.

You'll need just a few things: your favorite seeds, a trowel or other hand cultivator, straw, and garden fabric.

Select cold-hardy seeds suitable for winter growing. Good candidates include radishes, chard, and wild greens like purslane and sylvetta.

Build a cold frame for a smaller garden, or a hoop house for a larger one. Either of these two structures will provide the first and most important layer of protection for the winter garden. If you can't build or procure either of these two structures, a simple cover like cloth or straw will help to prolong the garden until the first sustained hard freeze occurs.

August is a good month to begin this work. Planting your winter garden early, before fall arrives, while the sun is still strong and the days are still relatively warm, is important. This will allow seeds to germinate and get a strong start on growing. Choose a warm, sunny location in the garden with good sun exposure to plant your seeds. This helps the cold frame, hoop house, or row cover work with the weather and keep plants warm.

When temperatures drop to freezing or below, cover your winter garden with layers of garden fabric—even if your seedlings are inside a cold frame or hoop house. If very cold nights are on the way, a temporary layer of straw will provide additional insulation. If this becomes necessary, lay the straw around the base of the plant and along the full length of your garden or window box. For gardeners in the far north (for zones, see Resources, page 265), additional heat sources inside the hoop house, acting like a woodstove, will ensure that the garden thrives into spring.

Plant growth occurs much more slowly during winter, so harvest accordingly. If gardening without the protection of a cold frame or hoop house in zone 8 or below, you can stave off the cold for only so long. Eventually, when those really cold nights roll in, you may have to accept winter and let it have its way.

HOW TO MAKE A KOKEDAMA

Kokedama, meaning "moss ball," is a style of Japanese bonsai that takes presentational aesthetics outside the box, literally. Kokedama are made by transferring a plant out of its pot and into a ball of soil held together with moss and string. String gardens take this tradition a step further by suspending these little green worlds in the air. We learned this project from our friend Taylor Patterson of Fox Fodder Farm, who showed us how to make our very own.

WHAT YOU'LL NEED

Newspaper

Gardening gloves (optional)

A selection of shade-loving plants with small root bases, such as ferns, ivies, cyclamens, creeping vines, miniature palms, or even herbs

A medium-sized bowl filled with room-temperature water

Sphagnum moss soaked in water for at least 30 minutes

Cotton thread

A 7:3 ratio of peat moss and bonsai soil (akedama) mixed together with enough water to achieve a claylike consistency

Sheet moss

Twine or string (natural and biodegradable)

DIRECTIONS

1. Either outdoors or in an indoor gardening space, lay out newspaper to catch any dirt, and set up your supplies. Knock the soil from the roots of your plants (wear gardening gloves if you like). You may have to tug the roots apart if they have wrapped around themselves in the pot. If so, gently scrunch them like you would when replanting and slowly massage the soil until it begins to loosen up.

2. Dip the roots in the bowl filled with room-temperature water.

3. Take enough sphagnum moss to wrap around the roots and squeeze out the excess water from the moss. Wrap the moss around the roots and bind together with cotton thread, finishing with a knot. The thread will eventually disintegrate and the roots will spread through the moss and into the soil.

4. Shape your bonsai and peat moss mixture into a ball about the size of a grapefruit—a small grapefruit for smaller plants and a larger grapefruit for larger plants.

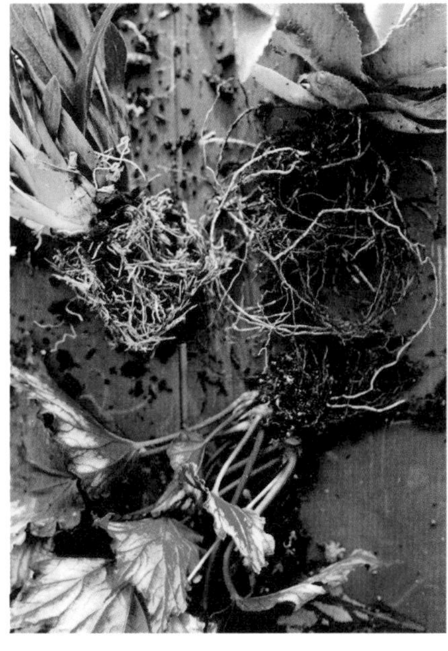

5. Once you've shaped the soil mixture into the appropriate-sized ball, break it in half and sandwich the roots between the two halves, reshaping the sphere around the roots, adding more soil to bind if necessary.

6. Cover the ball with a layer of sheet moss.

7. After you've wrapped the sheet moss, bind it with the biodegradable twine to keep it all from falling apart. Continue to wrap with twine until the ball feels secure and tie a knot, leaving enough string to hang the kokedama.

8. Pick a shade-friendly spot to mount your kokedama. It can be suspended from the ceiling, from a curtain rod, or in any well-ventilated space. Kokedama can be arranged as a singular plant or grouped to create a garden suspended in the air.

CARING FOR YOUR KOKEDAMA

Soak the kokedama for ten to fifteen minutes in water once a week (ferns need water twice a week). Let the plant drain in a sink until the water stops dripping before rehanging. With proper care, your kokedama should last for years.

WINTER

COOKING

DEXTER

WINTER

INGREDIENTS TO INSPIRE

Fruits

CHERIMOYA
GRAPEFRUIT
GUAVA
KIWI
KUMQUATS
LEMONS
LIMES
MANDARINS
OLIVES
ORANGES
PERSIMMONS
POMEGRANATES
POMELOS

Vegetables

AMARANTH
ARROWROOT
BELGIAN ENDIVE
BOK CHOY
BRUSSELS SPROUTS
BUTTERCUP SQUASH
CABBAGE
CELERIAC (CELERY ROOT)
CHICORY
COLLARD GREENS
DANDELION GREENS
DELICATA SQUASH
KALE
KOHLRABI
LEEKS
PARSNIPS
PEARL ONIONS
POTATOES
RUTABAGAS
SALAD SAVOY
SPINACH (LATE-SEASON)
SWEET DUMPLING SQUASH
SWEET POTATOES
TURNIPS
WASABI ROOT
WINTER SQUASH

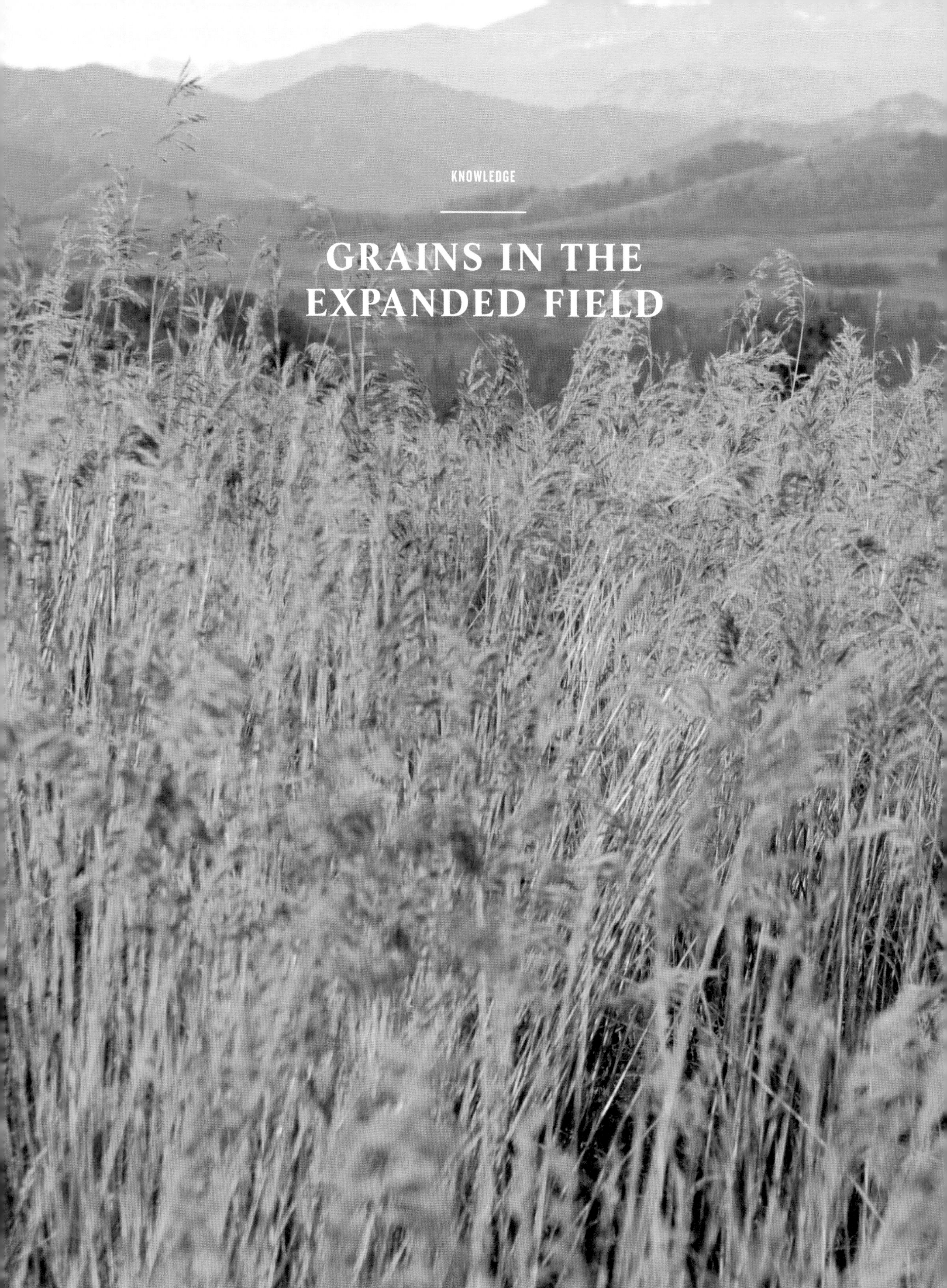

KNOWLEDGE

GRAINS IN THE EXPANDED FIELD

In winter when fresh vegetables are sparse, explore the rich and diverse world of another type of harvest: grain. Today grains are so readily available, we hardly consider their impact on the way we live. However, it was indeed the creation of agriculture and the resulting food surplus economy that allowed us to move beyond simply being hunters and gatherers.

Easily storable and shelf-stable, grains provide sustaining nutrition for people from all walks of life. Today, however, the demand for crops like soybeans and corn has evolved to include commercial production of everything from corn syrup to animal feed to nonfood industrial products. These demands have had an impact on the diversity of crops that farmers grow and, over time, created a deficit in soil nutrients. Farmers depend on crop rotation—alternating dissimilar crops per season—to naturally reestablish nutrients in the soil that the previous crop may have depleted. If farmers are planting to meet the demand for only a few crops, the nutrient quality of our soil may suffer.

We can help support our farmers and encourage the planting of diverse crops by voting with our dollars and purchasing a wider range of grains. Looking beyond traditional staple crops like corn, wheat, and soy will give the soil, as well as our bodies, greater nutritional variation. It will also ensure that ancient grains don't become extinct due to disuse.

When purchasing, look for whole-grain options. Grains—for both cereals and legumes—are the seed of the plant and can occur with or without the hull and fruit. "Whole grain" means that the entire seed kernel—bran, germ, and endosperm—is present in its original proportions, even if the grain has been minimally processed (cracked, crushed, rolled, etc.). Selecting a whole grain ensures that you are getting all the nutrients possible from the entire seed. Try some of these varieties and reap the benefits of grain, not just for your body, but for the health of our soil.

AMARANTH: An eight-thousand-year-old grain, amaranth was a sacred staple of Aztec culture. Legend has it that when the Spanish conquistador Hernán Cortés took over the region, he burned all the amaranth fields as a sign of his dominion. Amaranth is 14 percent protein and has no gluten. Its peppery flavor contributes to cereals, breads, and baked goods, as well as being delicious all on its own.

BARLEY: A sacred food to ancient Egyptians, who were often buried with necklaces of it strung together, the grain has been a staple to cultures around the world. Barley is very high in fiber and has an earthy, creamy flavor. It can be an excellent addition to soups and stews or complement to roast meats. Look for hulled, whole-grain barley and not pearled barley that has been processed to remove the bran.

EINKORN: Evidence of this ancient form of wheat can be found as far back as 7500 BCE, and some claim it is the oldest form of wheat—that is, an heirloom variety. Though out of fashion as of late, einkorn is making a comeback in the United States due to its drought-resistant growing capabilities and easy digestibility compared to other forms of wheat. Look for einkorn flour or berries to experience the nutritional benefits of increased fiber and protein.

FARRO: Most frequently associated with Italian cuisine, farro is gaining popularity in the United States as well. Also known as emmer wheat, farro is an ancient grain that was found planted throughout the Middle East. It is bouncy and resilient in texture and subtly nutty in flavor. It can be used as a substitute for arborio rice in risotto, for salads, or in hearty soups.

FREEKEH: This ancient Middle Eastern wheat has a unique harvesting process that creates its toasty, warm, and earthy taste. The wheat is harvested when the seeds are still yellow and soft, not yet dried and hard, and then dried in the sun. The entire harvest is set on fire so that the straw and hull burns away, but, due to the moisture content in the grain, the seed remains intact. The roasted wheat is then threshed and cracked before it is ready for consumption.

KHORASAN WHEAT: Known for its buttery flavor, khorasan wheat is an ancient grain from Egypt that is roughly twice as large as traditional wheat varieties. When grown in the United States and Canada, the brand name Kamut is used by producers to distinguish this particular variety.

MILLET: A type of small-seed grass, millet has been used in Indian cuisine for thousands of years as a flour to make traditional roti. It is also used to make beer in Taiwan, as well as porridge in Russian and Chinese cuisines. Millet is a gluten-free grain.

SPELT: Though once abundant, this variety of wheat fell out of favor as industrialized farming practices made other wheat options easier to grow. Spelt is more nutritionally dense than white, refined flour, and its light flavor makes it an easy substitute in most recipes.

TEFF: A staple of Ethiopian cooking, this tiny grain is roughly one millimeter in size (similar to a poppy seed) and has a deep flavor almost similar to that of molasses. Incorporate teff into cooked hot cereals, baked goods, and breads.

RECIPE

MAKE SAUERKRAUT

The process of making sauerkraut is somewhat magical. You take raw, frost-tolerant cabbage, add a little salt and a gentle massage, and this cool-weather staple is transformed into a probiotic-fortified, year-round condiment. Through the traditional preservation process of lacto-fermentation, healthy bacteria present on the raw vegetable and in the air grow on the raw vegetable and lower its pH, creating an environment too acidic for the toxins that cause botulism and mold. The luscious result is crisp, tangy, and a little sour—a bright complement to winter's heartier fare like roast meats, sausages, and rich soups.

This recipe was created by chef and food preservationist Michaela Hayes of Crock & Jar. It incorporates wild foraged chickweed and nigella seed (aka kalonji seed). If nigella is unavailable, caraway seeds—the traditional addition to sauerkraut—or fennel seeds can be used. For this recipe and all other fermentations, use whole spices and grind them in a dedicated coffee grinder.

INGREDIENTS

3 pounds green cabbage (one medium, heavy head)

2½ teaspoons nigella seed (optional)

1 tablespoon coarse sea salt

1 cup chickweed, chopped

EQUIPMENT

Large mixing bowl

Widemouthed half-gallon Mason jar with a lid

Plate

Jar

Towel

Rubber bands

Extra plastic container or jar for storing the sauerkraut in the fridge

Makes 1½ quarts

DIRECTIONS

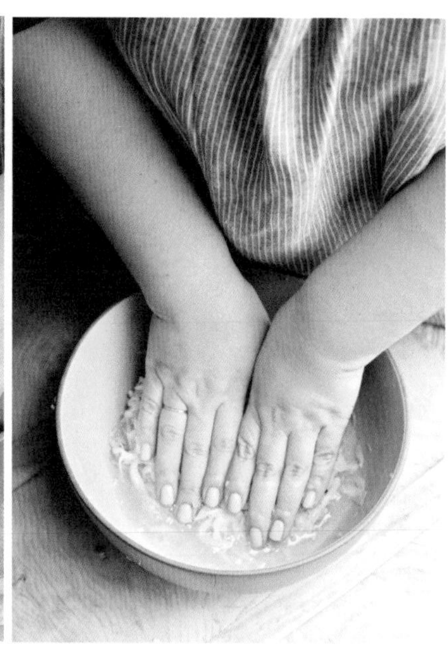

1. Remove the dark outer leaves and cut the cabbage into quarters. Remove the core and slice each wedge into ¼-inch-wide strips.

2. Place the cut pieces in a large mixing bowl, layering in salt and nigella seeds, if using, so that the cabbage begins to release its liquid.

3. Massage the cabbage to help the salt penetrate. Press down on the cabbage until it releases enough liquid to cover itself. This may take some effort. Press hard!

4. Weigh down the cabbage until it is entirely covered by liquid by placing a plate with a filled jar, weight, or can of beans on top. Any cabbage that is not submerged will rot. If after 24 hours the cabbage is not completely immersed in liquid, add a heavier weight.

5. Transfer the cabbage mixture to a jar. Place a weight directly on top of the cabbage mixture and cover the container with a kitchen towel and tighten with a rubber band.

6. Check the progress after 1 week; remove the weight, washing off any mold and removing any rotten bits. The cabbage below these spots is totally fine to eat. Taste it for sourness. Re-cover the cabbage if you want it even more tangy.

7. Check the sauerkraut once a week. Depending on your preference for sourness and texture, it should be ready 2 to 6 weeks from the date you began.

8. Once the kraut has become sour enough for your liking, put it in a clean container and store it in the refrigerator. This is a living food, so it should be consumed within 1 month.

RECIPE

MAKE KIMCHI AT HOME

Kimchi is the national dish of Korea, where babies are fed spoonfuls of it with rice as some of the first foods they consume. This pungent, fiery-red staple of fermented cabbage, spices, and other vegetables is incorporated into soups, noodles, and rice dishes and served as a side dish at many meals. Beyond its culinary importance, kimchi has been a significant part of Korean culture. Different regions of the country have developed unique recipes and techniques for the national dish, as well as seasonal variations. A far cry from the fairly standardized condiment we encounter at Western Korean restaurants, kimchi in its own country is a nuanced language unto itself.

Though kimchi is made throughout the year, November and December are especially high production months; large batches are made by friends, families, and neighbors in anticipation of the cold winter. Because of large quantities made during these months, kimchi has historically been stored in earthenware vessels called *onggi* and buried underground over the winter to ferment in a temperature-regulated environment.

Similar to the process used in making sauerkraut, kimchi takes advantage of the natural bacteria present in cabbage that facilitates lacto-fermentation, which lowers the vegetable's pH, creating an environment too acidic for toxins that cause botulism and mold. With kimchi, this process is particularly fizzy as airborne bacteria also contribute to the fermenting process, altering the flavor and texture of the kimchi over time.

Kimchi maker, cookbook author, and Mother-in-Law's Kimchi founder Lauryn Chun shared this recipe for winter kimchi with us. Try it incorporated into rice dishes, dipping sauces, noodles, or dumplings, or on its own as a condiment.

INGREDIENTS

2 heads of Napa cabbage

⅓ cup kosher salt

7 cloves garlic

2-inch knob of ginger

3 to 4 anchovies

3 tablespoons water

1 teaspoon sugar

3 tablespoons Korean chili powder (gochugaru)

5 scallions, chopped

EQUIPMENT

Large bowl

Plate

Weight (such as a can of beans or a small pot)

Colander

Food processor

Rubber gloves

Funnel

Tongs

2 quart-sized Mason jars

Shallow dish or bowl

Makes 2 quarts

DIRECTIONS

1. Cut the cabbage in half lengthwise. Discard the inner core of the cabbage and its heart. Cube the remaining cabbage into 1-inch squares, taking care to keep the pieces intact. Place the cabbage in a large bowl with at least 3 inches of headroom.

2. Add the salt to the cabbage and massage the mixture with your hands. Add water to cover the cabbage so that no bits of the vegetable are above water. Place a plate with a weight (a can of beans, for example) on top of the plate so that the cabbage is forced further under water, and allow the cabbage to brine overnight or for 10 to 12 hours.

3. Transfer the cabbage to a colander and allow the salt water to drain. Rinse the cabbage thoroughly.

4. While the cabbage is draining, prepare your spice paste. Combine the garlic, ginger, anchovies, water, sugar, and chili powder in a food processor and blend until a thick paste forms. If the mixture needs to be loosened, add more water. Add more chili powder for a spicier flavor.

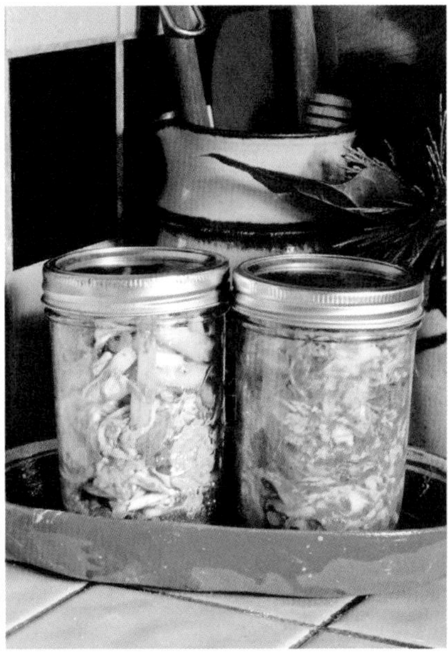

5. Mix the spice paste into the cabbage and add the scallions. Use rubber gloves to protect your hands as you massage each piece of cabbage with the spice mixture.

6. When the cabbage is sufficiently coated, use a funnel and tongs to pack the kimchi into your two jars. Leave 1 inch of headroom and loosely close the lids.

7. Place the two jars in a shallow dish or bowl and allow to ferment unrefrigerated for 3 to 5 days. Bubbles may appear as the fermentation process happens. The cabbage juice may ooze out of the top—this is a normal function of the fermentation process so the shallow dish or bowl will catch any bits that spill over.

8. After 3 to 5 days, transfer the kimchi to the refrigerator to slow down the fermentation process. It will mature and change in taste and is considered "ready" from this point on. The kimchi will keep in the refrigerator for up to 1 month.

WINTER

HOME & SELF-RELIANCE

WINTER

PREPARE YOUR HOME FOR THE SEASON

Notoriously, winter is the time to hunker down indoors. Take this opportunity to engage in projects like clothing repair or knitting—both of which have the added bonus of covering your lap to keep you warm as you work—reorganizing cupboards and closets, and tackling other indoor projects you may have been putting off. This is a good time to focus on and care for the living things in your life—houseplants, pets, and livestock need extra attention during this dry and cold time of year.

- ☐ **Mend old and worn clothes (see page 242 for instructions).**
- ☐ **Transform clothes that cannot be repaired into kitchen rags; save fabric scraps for future mending.**
- ☐ **Fill bird feeders with suet and birdseed for feathered friends during the snowy season (see page 240 for instructions).**
- ☐ **Break ice on ponds or set out a water dish for birds to drink from.**
- ☐ **Set out bowls of water on heaters or radiators if your indoor air becomes too dry.**
- ☐ **Incorporate houseplants into your living space to help clean the stuffy air.**
- ☐ **Open curtains and blinds to capture as much sunlight and warmth during the day as possible.**
- ☐ **Clean the leaves of your houseplants to make sure they photosynthesize to the best of their abilities in the dim winter light.**
- ☐ **Ensure that all animals have extra feed and bedding on cold nights.**
- ☐ **Force and harvest vegetables indoors (see page 158 for instructions).**
- ☐ **Start hardy vegetables indoors 8 weeks before the final frost date.**
- ☐ **Flag sugar maples for tapping as the temperature begins to rise above freezing.**
- ☐ **Place a sturdy, tough mat outside the house door to make sure all muck and snow stays where it belongs.**
- ☐ **Clean your teakettle with a boiling vinegar solution to remove mineral deposits.**

KNOWLEDGE

LIVE BY DOING

In the traditional American economy, we equate value with tangible currency; it is the barometer against which we know if something is significant, desirable, essential, or luxurious. But time, labor, meaningful objects, and knowledge all have associated value, too. So what would happen if we removed money from the equation and let value guide our economy?

Barter economies are one answer to this question. Barter economies have been in existence since early ancient cultures—and well before the invention of money. Today, barter exchanges may happen more frequently than you might think. Consider the new restaurant owner who has little start-up capital, but can readily trade future meals with contract workers, plumbers, or painters. Or, perhaps there is an agreement among friends to exchange help moving apartments for a homemade meal. Exchanges like these make up for a $12 billion annual economy, according to the International Reciprocal Trade Association.

Benefits of Barter Economies

Participating in a barter exchange creates a community-led, decentralized economy that reconfigures the supply and demand model—goods aren't manufactured to accommodate a perception of what the public needs or wants; they are exchanged when the need of an individual is present. In this way, barter economies reduce the amount of new goods created and the inevitable amount of discarded goods. In addition to easing strain on resources, barter economies help to bridge class divides—one person's labor or hour of work can be just as valuable as another's. These exchanges also allow businesses to "sell" goods to customers who are cash-poor.

What Can You Barter?

While simple exchange transactions can take place between any two people who share a like-minded philosophy (a haircut in exchange for fixing a broken radiator, for example), more complex barter clubs have developed to enhance your chances of trading for what you need. Each barter club has its own governing rules, so it is best to consult a local barter organization (see sidebar) to find out if any rules or exclusions apply. When first starting to barter, think broadly: you could exchange your time, pass on a skill, or educate someone about a subject on which you're an expert. Resources like houses, cars—even appliances—all have value. Allowing someone to use the resources you own is one way to trade. Another approach is to trade material goods that are no longer of use to you. You might not appreciate the value of what you have until you try to barter—one person's trash can be someone else's treasure after all.

Sharing Economies and Collaborative Consumption

Sharing economies are another form of bartering. In this type of model, assets are co-owned or rented by a group, as opposed to being owned by an individual. Making use of shared assets is easier today than ever before, thanks to sites like Craigslist, Airbnb, Uber, Lyft, and others. Technology has made these transactions seamless, incorporating social media as a form of establishing trustworthiness, peer-generated online reviews as a proof of credibility, and GPS mobility functions as tools to help source opportunities closest to you.

These economies allow individuals to provide services that were formerly in the exclusive domain of corporations. Now, individuals can be microentrepreneurs, creating businesses out of their own resources and communities out of their connections. With these economies, the more we are in tune with what we really need, the more we might find ourselves with things we really value.

ORGANIZATIONS TO HELP YOU GET STARTED

Bartering can be easy, and the right organizations can help you get started. Here are some options.

BARTER BUSINESS UNLIMITED

bbubarter.com

A barter economy network based in Connecticut that trades in everything from skilled labor to consumer goods.

BARTER NEWS WEEKLY

barternewsweekly.com

A weekly publication that reports on barter industry trends and news, and gives tips.

THE FREECYCLE NETWORK

freecycle.org

Organizes meet-up groups around the world to give and receive free goods, from clothing to furniture, and in doing so eases the pressure on landfills.

INTERNATIONAL RECIPROCAL TRADE ASSOCIATION

irta.com

A membership-based organization that supports barter transactions worldwide.

HELP COMMON BIRDS IN YOUR AREA THRIVE

Winter can be a trying time for our avian friends. Food and water sources become scarce as cold weather grips many parts of the world in winter months. Helping birds as they make their journey south for the winter can be as easy as knowing what foods they like to eat and how best to feed them.

There is perhaps no one who knows the ways of the winged like the Audubon Society. Geoff LeBaron, Christmas Bird Count Director for the United States' National Audubon Society, shares how to identify local birds in your area.

NORTHEAST UNITED STATES

- **AMERICAN ROBIN:** The quintessential early bird is a common sight on grassy lawns. Robins are popular for their warm orange breast, cheery song, and early appearance at the end of winter. They are commonly found in parks, suburbs, and moist woodlands in winter. Offer them mixed seeds.
- **BLUE JAY:** A common, large songbird with blue, white, and black plumage and a perky crest, the blue jay is generally very noisy and bold. Feed this commoner mixed seeds with millet.
- **DOWNY WOODPECKER:** North America's smallest and most widespread woodpecker is often seen in varied habitat around urban areas. It will readily come to suet, peanut butter, or seed feeders.

SOUTHEAST UNITED STATES

- **TUFTED TITMOUSE:** A little gray songbird with a short crest, round bill, and big black eyes, the tufted titmouse enjoys mixed seed and is a frequent visitor to feeders.
- **EASTERN BLUEBIRD:** A rare visitor to the feeder but a frequent birdbath bather, the eastern bluebird, which is predominantly blue, can be most easily identified by its orange throat and sides of neck and breast with a white lower belly. It can be enticed by a few mealy worms left on a platform feeder.
- **NORTHERN CARDINAL:** A perennial favorite songbird in urban shrubland, the male bird is red all over with a cone-shaped bill and crest while the female is more brown. In winter, cardinals will readily come to sunflower- and mixed-seed feeders, often in gender-specific flocks.

CENTRAL UNITED STATES

- **AMERICAN CROW:** Large all-black birds, with hoarse, cawing voices, crows are common sights in a variety of habitats ranging from open woods and empty beaches to town centers. They usually feed on the ground and eat almost anything but might especially enjoy a smattering of dried corn.
- **HARRIS'S SPARROW:** A songbird with restricted breeding range in far north-central Canada, its entire wintering range is in the U.S. central and southern Great Plains. The Harris's sparrow can be found in yards, usually on the ground under feeders in winter, where it enjoys mixed seeds.
- **WHITE-BREASTED NUTHATCH:** This small short-tailed acrobat climbs up and down trees and around tree trunks and branches. Nuthatches' white faces and breasts with black cap can be seen among leafy trees. Feed them mixed seeds.

NORTHWEST UNITED STATES

- **ANNA'S HUMMINGBIRD:** This is the common resident hummingbird of the northwest U.S. coast. The male's head and throat are deep red, while the female's show red flecks. The body is mostly green with grayish underparts. These birds may congregate at nectar feeders supplied in yards, especially in the winter months when fewer flowers are in bloom.
- **MOUNTAIN CHICKADEE:** This common songbird sprite of the western U.S. mountains can be encountered in mixed flocks in mountainside woodlands. It has white "eyebrows" and pale sides, with a black cap and throat. It readily visits feeders and enjoys suet, sunflower seeds, and peanut butter.
- **STELLER'S JAY:** The jay of the Rocky Mountains, this deep azure-blue bird with dusty gray-brown feathers readily visits yards of mountain retreats, dry shrublands, oak woodlands, and pinyon pine-juniper forests. This species may move to the lowlands during some winters—and to the feeders in the yards of flatlanders. Feed it mixed seeds with millet.

SOUTHWEST UNITED STATES

- **GREATER ROADRUNNER:** Looking and sounding nothing like the popular cartoon character, roadrunners are in fact large, predatory ground cuckoos. Frequently encountered along roadsides or in open desert scrublands, roadrunners will readily visit urban areas and yards as well—in search of not bird seed but small animals (lizards and snakes, small mammals, large insects, and even small birds) that consume waste seed under feeders.
- **SPOTTED TOWHEE:** A large sparrow of the U.S. West, spotted towhees can often be found in shrublands or on the ground under or near feeders. Males have gleaming black feathers on their head and neck, spotted and striped wings, and a white and rust belly. The females are more gray. Spotted towhees like mixed seeds.

GIVE CLOTHES A SECOND LIFE WITH SASHIKO EMBROIDERY

Our love of fast fashion has spiked the amount of clothing produced while reducing the cost per item so, theoretically, there is more to buy. But, according to a Secondary Materials and Recycled Textiles (SMART) report, 11.9 million tons of clothing in America goes unsold. Although 16 percent of those clothes are donated to charities or sold to developing countries, a staggering 84 percent wind up shredded and in landfills so as to protect a brand's value and limit the amount of a brand's clothing on the market. The cycle is maddening: amped-up production to create cheaper products, which creates an excess of product, which then needs to be destroyed to maintain brand value.

All factors considered—environmental impact on methods of fiber growth, chemical dye processing, and factory production—the ecological cost of making a new article of clothing can be pretty steep. In such a troubling context, picking up a needle and thread may seem like a decidedly hopeful act.

Perfectly broken-in jeans succumbing to a rip or tear, or a button missing from a blouse, is often the reason a favorite item of clothing gets sent packing. These problems have simple fixes with time-honored, and often beautiful, traditions of mending. This style of mending is taken from *sashiko*, a Japanese method of embroidery that was traditionally used by farmers and fishermen to reinforce work wear, beginning in the Edo period. The technique developed out of practicality—building up layers of fabric strengthened the garment and also made it warmer. In this method, rows of horizontal running stitches are used against the grain of the fabric to fortify a weakened area.

Because most work wear of the era was dyed the readily available indigo, *sashiko* has developed the particular aesthetic of white thread on deep blue cloth, which works particularly well for contemporary denim. Sewing with bold, contrasting threads like golden yellow, fuchsia, or eggplant can heighten this contrast and give your denim jeans a second life. If you prefer a subtler, almost invisible appearance, substitute a colored thread that matches your garment where we have used white.

WHAT YOU'LL NEED

Measuring tape

A patch of fabric 1 inch larger in diameter than your hole

Scissors

Sewing pins

Thread, white or a bold color such as fuchsia or yellow

Needle

DIRECTIONS

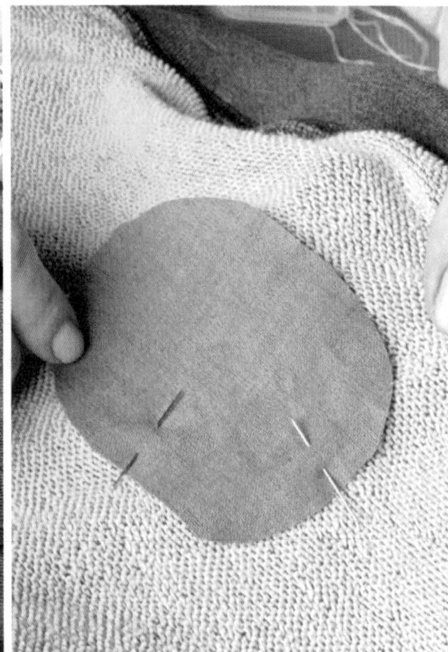

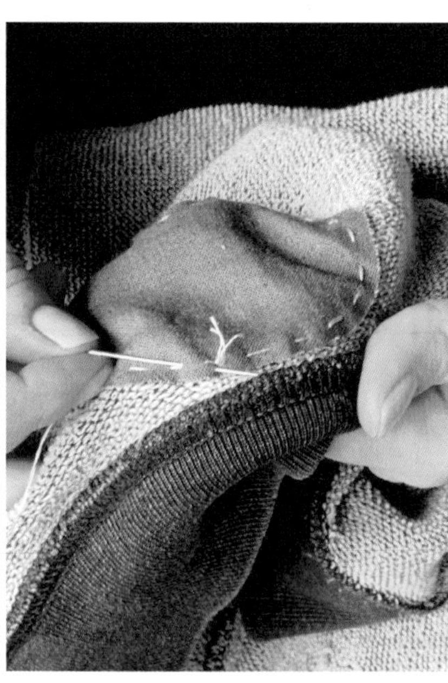

1. Measure the patch against the hole in the fabric that you want to repair.

2. Cut the patch at least 1 inch larger than the hole. Round the corners of your patch to limit fraying.

3. Turn your jeans or garment inside out and pin your patch in place over the affected area.

4. Thread your needle. Using a running stitch (a basic over-under stitch), tack the patch down by sewing along the perimeter of the patch in a continuous line. Knot your thread and cut it.

5. Inverse your garment so the front side is showing.

6. Using a small running stitch, sew rows, crosses, or another pattern onto the visible side of the garment. Knot your thread and cut it. The patch is now fastened. Further design work can be done at this point, or the garment can be ready to wear.

WINTER

BEAUTY & HEALING

KNOWLEDGE

A SEASONAL APOTHECARY

The cold of winter can make us feel sluggish and low. Across the country, we receive less sunlight in the winter, which diminishes our vitamin D supply. Our retreat indoors makes us more susceptible to catching common colds and the flu, while colder weather in some parts of the country means dry or irritated skin. Take preventive measures to ward off sickness with plants like elder, soothe yourself with a hot cup of lavender tea, and comfort and warm your body with the following herbs.

HERBS TO COMBAT SICKNESS

Chamomile
Anti-inflammatory; excellent at promoting deep restfulness and helping with insomnia. Use as an herbal bath or tea.

Elder
Use in combination with echinacea for immune support. Use as a tincture or tea.

HERBS TO COMFORT AND SOOTHE

Hawthorn
Helps soothe feelings of loss, sadness, and seasonal affective disorder (SAD). Use as a tea—it's wonderful in combination with lemon balm.

Lavender
Calming and relaxing to the nervous system; helps relieve tension, insomnia, and headaches. Use as a tea or tincture, or externally as an infused oil.

Oats
Helps heal dry, chapped skin when used in a bath or as soap.

HERBS TO WARM AND STIMULATE

Cayenne
Capsaicin stimulates blood flow and releases endorphins. Use as a culinary herb to bring heat to the body.

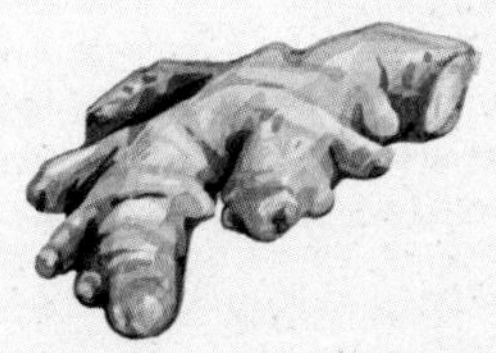

Ginger
Improves circulation; aids in digestion and helps to relieve nausea; a decongesting herb for colds. Use as a tea with lemon and honey or as a culinary herb.

Rosemary
Has an uplifting effect; helps to relieve minor headaches. Use as a culinary herb or as a tincture.

Sage
Aids in sluggish digestion that can happen in cooler months. Use as a culinary herb.

MEDITATING IN NATURE

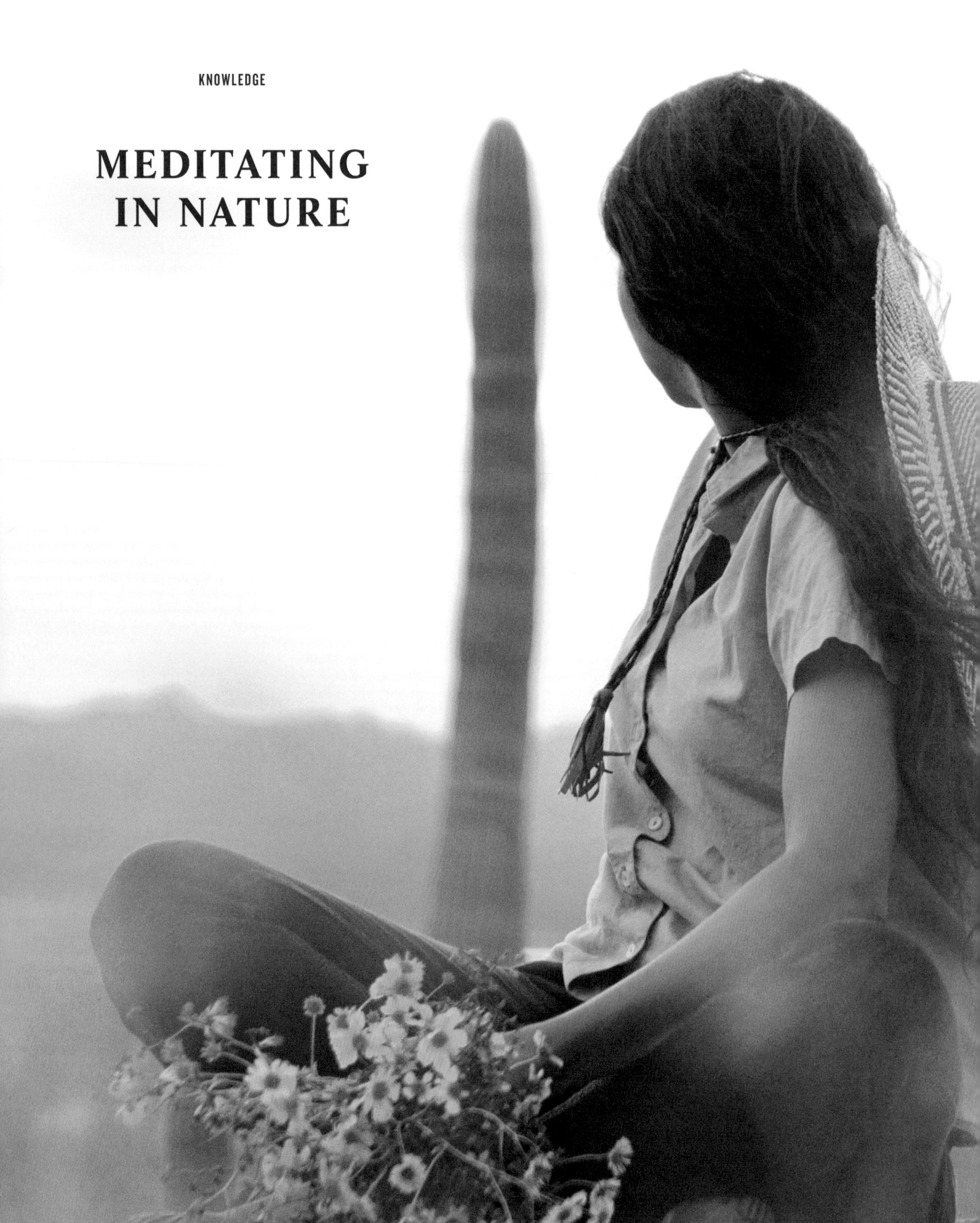

We take it for granted today that meditation may help reduce anxiety and improve quality of life. Yoga has become familiar to most and a weekly or even daily practice for many. We know what a mantra is, and chances are we've all made at least one attempt at an "om."

But, like all diasporic cultural movements, what seems commonplace today was rare at one point. Meditation as we now know it in Western culture owes much of its renown to Maharishi Mahesh Yogi, founder of Transcendental Meditation in the 1960s. It started as one man's vision and became a global empire and eventual movement, teaching a reported 5 million people the Transcendental Meditation technique—a nonreligious, mantra-based meditation, which is taught by trained teachers around the world. Since the maharishi's initial teachings, shades of his meditation practice have penetrated into the cultural vernacular, creating intentional communities, political parties, education and architecture programs, organic farms, and even its own currency.

Though the guru passed away in 2008, his technique lives on today, practiced and taught around the world by people like David Lynch, a creator of his own foundation that teaches Transcendental Meditation to at-risk groups like prisoners, inner city youth, and women who have suffered trauma (see Resources, page 265).

There are myriad methods of calming the mind and gaining focus. We like to practice in the great outdoors using a simple breathing technique. Here's how to do it.

Situate yourself in a quiet environment where you will be uninterrupted for at least twenty minutes. Look for a space with minimal sensory stimulation. A tranquil garden or unpopulated outdoor space are both good options, but a quiet room will do the trick, too.

Sit or lie in a comfortable position. Legs crossed with hands resting on knees is a common one, as is lying down on your back with limbs relaxed and palms turned upward. Find a position that works for you.

Begin by breathing in for five counts, holding that breath for four counts, and then exhaling for six counts. Keep your own pace and don't worry about how quickly or slowly you are breathing. Just focus on keeping the 5-4-6 pattern.

As thoughts enter your mind, acknowledge them, and then observe them recede as you continue to breathe and count.

If there is physical sensation, acknowledge it and then allow the sensation to recede back into your breathing.

Continue breathing in the 5-4-6 pattern for as long as you can; build up your time gradually. Begin by practicing for five minutes, then increase to twenty minutes or more as you find a rhythm, environment, and time of day that is best for you.

DIY

HOW TO MAKE A CALMING CALENDULA BALM

A hardy member of the marigold family, calendula is a favorite in many an herbalist's medicine cabinet. This *wunder* plant has been used for centuries in pharmacological, as well as culinary and aesthetic, applications. The golden, edible petals are a gorgeous addition to soups, salads, or teas, and when used as a natural dye, calendula imparts a warm saffron glow to fabrics.

But calendula's true genius lies in its medicinal properties. Plants give sensory signals of their capabilities, and calendula's sticky petals seem to almost ooze a healing serum. It is perhaps their tacky, adhesive feel that first gave herbalists clues to the flower's anti-inflammatory and antihemorrhagic qualities. When applied directly to a cut, as was commonly done when dressing injuries in the American Civil War, calendula petals are known to help bind and mend a wound. When incorporated into a healing ointment, as in this recipe, a calendula salve can help soothe and moisturize dry winter skin and reduce the irritation of sensitive skin. Our friend Marjory Sweet shared this recipe with us.

WHAT YOU'LL NEED

1 cup calendula petals, fresh or dried (see Resources on page 265 for where to buy)

1 cup olive oil (no need to use your finest cooking oil; a basic variety will do)

½ cup shaved or grated beeswax

10 drops essential oil, such as lavender, citrus, or rosemary

EQUIPMENT

Large glass Mason jar

Stainless-steel pot

Fine-mesh sieve

Cheesecloth

Glass mixing bowl

Double boiler

Whisk

Funnel

Several small, sterilized glass jars

Makes 1 cup

DIRECTIONS

1. Combine the petals and olive oil in a Mason jar and steep in direct sunlight for 2 weeks.

2. To make the salve, transfer the mixture to a nonreactive stainless-steel pot and bring to a simmer over low heat for 2 hours.

3. While the mixture is simmering, line a fine-mesh sieve with cheesecloth and set it over a glass mixing bowl.

4. Remove the mixture from the heat and strain the petals through the cloth. Use your hands to wring out as much liquid as possible from the cheesecloth. Set the glass bowl of oil extract aside.

5. Using a double boiler, place the wax over low heat and watch carefully as it begins to melt. Stir occasionally and be careful not to let it overheat, burn, or bubble. Melting should take about 5 minutes.

6. When the wax is completely melted and smooth, immediately whisk the oil into it, and continue whisking until smooth. If wax chunks form, raise the heat and whisk until smooth.

7. When the mixture is thoroughly smooth and combined, add the essential oil and stir to blend.

8. Using a funnel and a steady hand, transfer the mixture into clean, sterilized jars. Amber apothecary jars work best, as they reduce exposure to light, which can weaken your salve. When stored in a cool place out of direct sunlight, such as a bathroom cabinet, the salve should keep for 1 year.

WINTER

WILDERNESS

IS FT 14 691

KNOWLEDGE

EATING WINTER PLANTS IN THE WILD

Just because it's winter doesn't mean that delicious, wild edibles aren't waiting for you. It's incredible just how many plants and fruits are growing beneath the frost during the colder months. On your next walk through the woods or while on a cool-weather campout, keep your eyes peeled for some of the treats that winter has to offer.

CATTAILS

Bet you didn't know that cattails, the staple of any good pond or lake, are a wilderness lover's best friend. This amazing plant can provide fuel for heat. (Just light that cute fuzzy top on fire.) You can also use it as cover on a debris shelter and, yup, it's food, too. The cattail's nine-foot stalks are the edible bits with a mild, pleasing flavor and aroma.

CHICKWEED

Chickweed is one of the hardiest plants that grows in both heat and cold, sun and partial shade. It can be found in sunny spots almost anywhere in the Northern Hemisphere. When eaten raw, the plant has a sharp but not unpleasant taste. When cooked, it has a flavor like that of leafy greens, making it a great partner for onion, garlic, and potatoes.

PERSIMMON

Persimmons are one of the most widely planted trees in the world. They're not hard to spot, with their dark- colored, rugged bark and fragrant bright-orange fruit, which lingers long after the shiny oval-shaped leaves have succumbed to the cold. You can find them in the woods randomly or on the edge of cultivated properties. The unripe fruit has an astringent taste, so to ensure a sweet treat, make those that have already fallen from the tree your snack.

WATERCRESS

Foraged watercress tastes far different from what you might buy in the grocery store. Wild watercress has an unexpected peppery flavor. Find watercress growing in bunches deep into the winter months near bodies of water. If you're in a slightly warmer climate, you'll be able to spot its little white flowers from the shore. Beware: While the water may look just fine, it could be contaminated. Toxins and parasites can easily be passed to the watercress from the water it's growing in. If you're unsure if the water source is up to snuff, clip only the leaves above the waterline. Better to be safe than sorry.

WILD ONION

Often considered an invasive species, wild onions can be found growing almost everywhere from lawns to roadsides. They look a lot like chives with thin, dark green, circular stalks that end in a white bulb at the base. You'll instantly know you've got a wild onion by the aroma that fills the air after you uproot it. All parts of the wild onion are edible, so don't hesitate to dig in.

SKILL

TRAVEL BY THE SUN AND STARS AND NEVER GET LOST AGAIN

With modern technology at our disposal, getting lost in the woods can be no big deal. Cell phone, anyone? But occasionally, gadgets get broken, batteries die, or we're hiking out of range. Then what? Being able to find your way out of a sticky situation is a wilderness skill worth having. So, whether it's for fun or because you are truly lost (heaven forbid), here's how to navigate when the sun is high in the sky or when stars are lighting up the night.

Navigating by the Sun

On a clear day or a partially cloudy one, the sun can help get you back on track. Here's what you need to know: The sun rises in the east and sets in the west. If you can remember this, then you'll be able to use the sun's location to figure out the time of day, as well as your general position.

1. Place a stick in the ground.

2. Find a pebble and place it at the end of the stick's shadow. In fifteen minutes, the earth will have rotated and the shadow will have moved.

3. Place another pebble at the shadow's new position.

4. The line between the two stones will be pointed along the east-west axis, allowing you to point yourself in the right direction.

Navigating by the Stars

1. Before you head outside, do an Internet search or download the app Star Walk to your phone to familiarize yourself with the basic outline of the night sky. Having a rough idea of the constellation landscape will make the task of finding your way back to civilization a breeze.

2. Once you are lost, locate the Big Dipper. The seven stars that make up this formation are easy to spot, as together they form the outline of a soup ladle.

3. While other stars are in motion, the North Star, also known as Polaris, neither rises nor sets. The Earth's axis is always pointed directly at it. To locate this star, draw an imaginary line between the two stars Merak and Dubhe, These two form the outer edge of the Big Dipper's ladle. Follow your line until you hit a brighter, bigger star. This will be Polaris. With it, a lost traveler can judge the other directions (south, east, west), making it possible to stay oriented as you work your way back to civilization.

4. If it's too cloudy out to locate the North Star, here is another great trick. Place two sticks in the ground roughly a yard apart. Pick any star in the night sky and line it up with the tops of both sticks. Now wait for the Earth to begin its rotation. If the star shifts left, you're facing north. If the start shifts right, you're headed south. If it sinks, you're headed west. If it rises, you're facing east.

5. Pick a landmark in the distance to follow until you reach your destination.

EXPLORING HOT SPRINGS

Our world has water all across its surface and within its first layer of crust. Below this, the Earth is literally bubbling over with heat. This leads to geothermally heated groundwaters that take the shape of geysers, fumaroles, and our favorite, hot springs. What's the difference? If the water is so incredibly hot that it builds up an immense amount of pressure, it's a geyser. If only steam is released, it's a fumarole, and if it's a pool of water, it's a hot spring. While the former is fun to watch, it's the latter you'll want to enjoy. Hot springs are best experienced after vigorous activity. Their warm waters and high mineral content are, according to Chinese medicine, a boon to general well-being. Here are three experiences that offer not only great hikes but also one-of-a-kind springs.

Landmannalaugar, Iceland

Iceland has many pools of note, including the tourist attraction the Blue Lagoon. Rather than duke it out with hundreds of visitors, head off the beaten path to Landmannalaugar—"the people's pools." The springs sit at the edge of the Laugahraun lava field and are best enjoyed after a hike along the area's famous trails, which rest against the backdrop of Iceland's iconic orange-tinted mountains.

Ma'In Hot Springs, Jordan

The Dead Sea has long been revered for its healing properties. This spring in particular has a rich history, as it is believed to be the place where Salome danced her wicked dance and John the Baptist suffered his beheading. Today, there is a modern spa on the site that will allow you to soak in waters that originated in Jordan's highlands, then passed through the Wadi Zarqa Ma'in valley and deep fissures of the Earth. After a hike through the nearby canyon or mountains, you'll be glad to submerge yourself in the waters imbued with a range of minerals at levels not found anywhere else on the planet.

Tongass National Forest, Alaska

This remote hot springs is accessible only by canoe. But don't worry, you would not be roughing it. This area is home to a plethora of endangered species and just over seventy thousand people. Once there, you'll find yourself face-to-face with two hot tubs and an enclosed structure to be used as a changing room, kindly provided by the National Parks Service. During holidays, it can get a bit crowded, but the majority of the time it'll be just you, the moose, and epic scenery.

RESOURCES

APOTHECARY SUPPLIES

Mountain Rose Herbs
mountainroseherbs.com

CRYSTALS

Dave's Down to Earth Rock Shop
davesrockshop.com

GROWING ZONES

United States Department of Agriculture (USDA)
usda.gov

USDA Plant Hardiness Map
planthardiness.ars.usda.gov

IKEBANA

The Art of Arranging Flowers, by Shozo Sato

Ikebana International
ikebanahq.org

MAKING CHEESE

Culture: The Word on Cheese
culturecheesemag.com

MEDITATION

David Lynch Foundation
davidlynchfoundation.org

WORKING WITH BEES

Beekeeping 101
almanac.com/home-pets-family/beekeeping-blog

Bees for Beginners, by E. H. Taylor

ACKNOWLEDGMENTS

A big, warm thank-you to our fellow bookmakers: Molly Marquand, Holly Exley, Krysta Jabczenski, and Claire Cottrell. Thank you for bearing with us as we navigated this big, bad project. Thank you to our significant others, Matthew Maddy and Karl Briedrick, who get lots of gratitude for putting up with the madness. And forever thank you to Rabbit for teaching us all.

We are forever in debt to the experts who shared their wisdom, insight and time: Brenda Brock, Dan Barber, David Lynch, April Bloomfield, Christina Tosi, Eloise Augustyn, Christy Matson, Deb Soule, Marjory Sweet, Lauryn Chun, Susanne Ameln, Kate Sennert, Rory Gunderson, Michelle Kamerath, Adrian Shirk, Leif Hedendal, Michaela Crock, Linda Rodin, Rosemary Gladstar, Siggi Hilmarsson, Dieu Donné, Sarah Buscho, Marina Storm, Rachel Budde, Melissa Kelly, Hall Newbegin, Tata Harper, Beatrice Valenzula.

Finally, Kari Stuart. You're a total badass.

PHOTOGRAPHY CREDITS

All photographs are by Krysta Jabczenski and Claire Cottrell except for those listed below.

Pages 10, 20–21, 29, 31, 56–57, 60, 154, 164, 252: Abbye Churchill
Pages 24, 80, 96–97, 122–23, 130, 134–35: Rafael Rios
Page 26: Jody Rogac
Page 39: Todd Jordan
Page 43: Yossy Arefi
Page 71: Jim, the photographer
Pages 74, 76, 77: Osma Harvilahti
Page 92: Halfrain
Page 114: Jardin Botanico de Madrid
Page 116: Tyler Kolhoff
Pages 126, 127: Bobby Doherty
Page 138: Andrés Nieto Porras
Page 140: Luisa Peliper
Page 156: Anouck Bertin
Pages 198, 199: Tim Stanford
Pages 217, 218, 219: Rory Gunderson
Pages 220–21: Nicholas Haggard

INDEX

ABOUT THE AUTHORS

Celestine Maddy, founder and publisher of *Wilder,* and **Abbye Churchill**, *Wilder*'s editorial director, have spent the last five years inspiring and helping readers of their magazine connect with the great outdoors. Maddy is a longtime gardener who splits her time between Los Angeles and New York growing strange plants in her backyard, hiking with her husband, and hanging out in the corners of the Internet. Churchill is a writer, artist, and herbalist living in Chicago who spends her free time traveling the world in search of unique natural experiences.